For those longing to memorialize a love
an invaluable tool from a compassionate
pressures of time and integrity. Easy-to-r
tips, and perfect for those in a hospice set

Laurel Goodrick, LGPC, NCC, Bereavement Counselor

As a funeral director, a eulogy that has been delivered leaving survivors laughing through their tears is not just representative of a life well lived but also of a life best expressed. This book will help others to tap into the very emotions we think we should be kept under wraps when talking about life. *Good Words* captures the necessity to accurately detail a life, while balancing the use of feelings and reason. Well done!

Kathleen Santivasci, Mortician, McComas Funeral Home, PA

An excellent resource to help you with one of life's most difficult tasks—to honor a loved one through a eulogy.

Charles F. Evans, Jr., President, Evans Funeral Chapel and Cremation Services

Dr. Hewett has done a magnificent job in giving us practical tools necessary to tackle the emotionally laden task of writing a eulogy. She has created a user friendly resource in which each chapter of *Good Words* addresses a different facet of eulogy writing, making it easy for the reader to quickly find the specific information he is seeking. Full of examples, suggestions and points to consider, this much needed resource addresses every aspect of the eulogy, from how to begin to the moment the eulogy is given. In the chapter about children, Dr. Hewett sensitively addresses how to write a eulogy for a child who has passed away, as well as how to include children and adolescents in writing and speaking a eulogy. This little book fills a big need for anyone faced with the task of writing a eulogy.

Dr. Richard Ottenstein, CEO Workplace Trauma Center, Certified Trauma Specialist

Good Words

Memorializing Through a Eulogy

Beth L. Hewett, Ph.D.

WESTBOW®
PRESS
A DIVISION OF THOMAS NELSON
& ZONDERVAN

Updated 2014
Previously published by Grief Illustrated Press, 2010

WestBow Press books may be ordered through booksellers or by contacting:

WestBow Press
A Division of Thomas Nelson & Zondervan
1663 Liberty Drive
Bloomington, IN 47403
www.westbowpress.com
1 (866) 928-1240

ISBN: 978-1-4908-3804-5 (sc)
ISBN: 978-1-4908-3805-2 (hc)
ISBN: 978-1-4908-3803-8 (e)

Library of Congress Control Number: 2014909387

Printed in the United States of America.

WestBow Press rev. date: 08/22/2014

Acknowledgements

My deep thanks for the assistance and support of the following people: Daryl L. Lengyel, my much-loved mother who gave me the idea for this book; Susan L. Pahl, my dearest friend who offered many improvements to the draft and allowed me to memorialize her beloved father Herb; Christina Lengyel, my talented niece who offered her own experiences and edited my words; Dom John Farrelly, O.S.B., my spiritual advisor who always expressed belief in this book; Jean Dietz Moss, my teacher and friend who encouraged me; and Charlotte Robidoux, my dear friend and desktop publishing expert. My special thanks goes to Paul L. Hewett, Jr., Russell J. Hewett, Paul L. Hewett, Daniel Hewett, William Hewett, W. Russell Carmichael, Sherrill Hummell, Violet Slobodinsky, William Lyons, Mark Slaughter, and Mary Carol and Chuck DiPaula—all of whom helped me to know their own loved ones so that their eulogies could be written.

I very much appreciate the time and energy offered by Laurel Goodrick, Kathleen Santavisci, Charles Evans, Jr., and Richard Ottenstein—each of whom read drafts of this book and offered comments that vastly improved my efforts. I especially appreciate my gracious editor, Robbin Warner, Ph.D.

Portions of this text—either verbatim or paraphrased—were published originally as a chapter in *Sizing Up Rhetoric*, edited by David Zarefsky and Elizabeth Benacka (Waveland Press, 2008); see "The Eulogy: Grief and Wisdom of the Ancients," pp. 90-100. I thank both the Rhetoric Society of America and Waveland Press for allowing me to reuse this material.

Dedication

This book is dedicated to the memory of my deceased loved ones: my brother George J. Lengyel †2000, grandmother Anna Lengyel †2001, father George J.C. Lengyel †2001, mother-in-law Catherine Hewett †2002, sister Katherine M. Weis †2010, father-in-law Paul L Hewett †2011, and spiritual advisor Fr. John Farrelly, O.S.B. †2011. May they rest in the peace of God's loving arms while we remember them with good and healing words.

Contents

Guide to Using This Book

In the Case of a Sudden Death

If you have just experienced the sudden death of a loved one and want to write a eulogy, please read chapter 3 first. Then, use appendix C's brief Eulogy Writing Guide to help you draft the eulogy. If you desire, this appendix can be copied or removed from the back of the book and used in conjunction with chapter 3. Finally, chapter 5 provides tips for reading the eulogy effectively.

In the Case of Pre-Writing or Post-Writing the Eulogy

Consider reading the entire book before beginning to write if:

- You're writing the eulogy from a hospice or hospital setting;
- You otherwise have more time to prepare for the funeral or memorial ceremony; or,
- You're writing the eulogy after these ceremonies are past.

To help you in using this book, the table of contents provides both the chapter titles and the major subjects covered in each chapter.

Introduction

I learned about death the hard way. During 2000 through 2002, I lost my older brother, paternal grandmother, father, and mother-in-law—all in less than two years. Their deaths sent shock waves through me and my family. We reeled with grief. Since then, both my father-in-law and sister have died.

These weren't the first deaths in my experience, but they were the most life-changing and emotionally powerful. Death became a new companion. Once vague and abstract, death became real in my life.

And why not? Once we're born, the only other certainty of life is that one day we and all of our loved ones will die. We don't like to think about death, but every year, as many as 2,500,000 Americans die. That's approximately 8.5% of the total United States' population. The chances are good that each year we'll know at least one—if not more—of these people. As we grow older, of course, our losses multiply and we find ourselves seeking ways to integrate these losses into our lives.

Many of our loved ones are remembered and mourned in formal funeral and memorial ceremonies. For people who experience the healing of such ceremonies, there is a growing trend toward personalizing them. Personal touches set the stage for understanding the deceased as unique.

The eulogy is another way to personalize the ceremony. It is an ancient method of memorializing that is still used in many cultures, religions, and nationalities. The eulogy is a short speech praising and blessing the life of the deceased. The word "eulogy" comes from Greek and means "good words." Sometimes, "eulogy" is translated as "praise" and "blessing." The good words of a eulogy can open up the mourning process for the bereaved and grieving.

Unfortunately, people often feel uncomfortable with writing or delivering these good words. Few of us express confidence that our loved one is being honored with fitting words. Instead, we express fear, anxiety, or an inability to write or to speak publicly. Sadly, at a time when we naturally feel torn apart and inarticulate from grief, we also may feel burdened by a perception that we "can't write," and therefore can't do justice to our loved ones.

One way around this dilemma is to have someone else write the eulogy. For example, through the Internet one can find people who create ceremonies and those who write eulogies for a fee. While these eulogy writers provide thoughtful eulogies in a short time, they don't know our loved ones. The eulogy will never be quite as rich and as personal as one that we can write for people we know and love. For this reason, whenever possible, I urge the bereaved to have someone who knew the deceased write the eulogy.

A genuine need to pay tribute to a loved one through a eulogy may create a tension between desire and discomfort. This tension makes the difficult day of the funeral still more difficult, adding an unnecessary burden to an already stressful time. As eulogy writers (or eulogists), we may be afraid that the gathered people will judge us on the words, evaluating whether we have sufficiently honored the deceased. At the same time, we want to infuse the eulogy with dignity, respect, and deep feeling for our loved ones. In these situations, we need special support. *Good Words: Memorializing Through a Eulogy* was written to provide that support.

This book explains why eulogies, both traditional and contemporary, add to the public sense of mourning provided by a funeral or other memorial service. In fact, all of the elements needed for a powerful eulogy already have been provided by ancient writers like the Greek philosopher Aristotle and the Roman orator Cicero. Using their ideas as a basis, this book outlines simple, time-honored, and proven steps for developing and presenting a memorable eulogy.

4

Personal Touches

Mementos of the deceased person's:

- 🐝 Life
- 🐝 Spirituality
- 🐝 Career/s
- 🐝 Honors
- 🐝 Hobbies

Example ways to honor the deceased person's life:

- 🐝 Scout or military honor guards
- 🐝 Photo montages and videos
- 🐝 Letters from students
- 🐝 Live choir or band music

Because writing a eulogy almost always occurs when we're deeply moved by painful emotions, *Good Words: Memorializing Through a Eulogy* organizes these steps by the most-to-least important details. You only need to read the chapters that seem useful to you. This book will help if writing is difficult for you or if you have little time to write. You'll find in it specific, direct guidance for preparing simple, effective eulogies. This guidance, which is fully explained in the book's chapters, is summarized in appendix C's brief "Eulogy Writing Guide" that can be removed from the back of the book. If you prefer to speak off-the-cuff, you'll find tips for preparing notes.

Writing the eulogy is only part of the process. Someone (often the writer but not always) must read the eulogy. Therefore, this book also offers advice for delivering the eulogy with confidence despite the emotional stress of the funeral ceremony.

I wrote *Good Words: Memorializing Through a Eulogy* because of my own personal experiences with both sudden and anticipated death. I have come to understand the eulogy's importance in recognizing and celebrating a loved one's life. As an experienced bereavement support facilitator, facilitator trainer, and grief coach, I have developed memorial services, grief seminars, and healing retreats for the bereaved. As a college writing instructor, I have coached many writers who have different skill levels. My experiences will help you to write a eulogy that genuinely honors your loved one.

What You'll Find in This Book

This book is written for anyone who needs or wants to write a eulogy. If you're doing so for the first time, *Good Words: Memorializing Through a Eulogy* will help you through the process. If you're in the process of re-memorializing or tuning up a previously written eulogy, this book is equally helpful. Whether you're preparing a traditional or a contemporary eulogy, understanding the nature of a traditional eulogy will aid you in developing a powerful memorial to pay tribute to the deceased in a way that the funeral attendees will appreciate.

Good Words: Memorializing Through a Eulogy addresses your needs as a eulogy writer by helping you decide

- What to say
- How to organize your ideas
- How to phrase them gracefully, powerfully, and even humorously when appropriate

This book also provides suggestions for delivering the eulogy in the high-stress environment of the funeral. Finally, it addresses such special circumstances as writing and delivering a eulogy when the relationship with the deceased has been a difficult one, developing the eulogy for multiple speakers, using writing or thoughts of the deceased, considering the special needs of children, and revising the eulogy after the funeral should you desire to do so.

Chapters 1 and 2 explain what a eulogy is and why it's so helpful for mourners to hear it. Chapters 3 and 4 explain what to say in the eulogy and how to organize it. **If time is very short, first read chapter 3 and use the "Eulogy Writing Guide" appendix C for additional help**. Chapter 5 outlines strategies for delivering the formal traditional eulogy. Chapter 6 considers the special needs of both the eulogy for deceased children and the inclusion of children in a funeral or memorial ceremony. Chapter 7 explains how to polish your eulogy as a lasting memorial. Finally, chapter 8 explains how eulogies may be viewed in various religious backgrounds and how to create more contemporary eulogy forms.

Various chapters will guide you to appendix A for model eulogies, which were written for loved ones like yours. They can be found both within the text and cross-referenced with the appendix. Appendix B contains model poems that you can use in honoring your loved one if a traditional eulogy doesn't seem to be appropriate to your situation. Appendix C is a brief guide for writing a eulogy that can help you in your writing. Also, look for textboxes and examples that illustrate ideas and writing methods and that highlight various skills.

> **If you're pressed for time:**
>
> ⚹ Read chapter 3 for how to figure out what to say in the eulogy.
>
> ⚹ Read chapter 5 for how to deliver it.
>
> ⚹ Use appendix C, "Eulogy Writing Guide," to help you stay focused.
>
> When your eulogy is drafted (and if you have time), read through the other chapters that may meet your needs

Personal Thoughts

On a very personal note, I started planning this book in 2000 when my brother George and his co-pilot were killed in an ultra-light plane crash. His was the first eulogy I wrote. Despite the horrendous shock of George's death and the deep grief surrounding me, I used the principles in this book to write a moving eulogy that included input from his wife, children, parents, siblings, and friends. These principles helped me think about writing when I was otherwise disconnected from the rest of the world.

Contrast that with the experience of another family in a similar crisis of unexpected, accidental death. Without an understanding of the healing power of a traditional eulogy, it's possible that their written tribute might express their anger, shock, and pain in a blaming sort of way. If their speech reflects anger and pain and doesn't involve good words of praise, blessing, or honor, it essentially won't pay tribute to the loved one like a more traditionally guided eulogy can. In fact, it can make the gathered mourners uncomfortable and miss the opportunity for mourning and celebrating the deceased person's life in positive and emotionally rewarding ways.

Writing a speech at any time can be anxiety provoking. Writing a eulogy, which is both personal and public, can raise anxiety even higher—particularly when the family has mixed feelings about a loved one's actions and manner of death.

There are few "must do" rules for eulogies. There are, however, some tried and true guidelines that can help us when we're shocked and grieved yet needing to find good words for our loved ones.

My hope is that *Good Words: Memorializing Through a Eulogy* will help ease your stress. I send you my best wishes for peace during this challenging time.

Chapter 1

What Is a Eulogy?

What a Eulogy Is

A eulogy, also called a funeral oration, is a speech that praises and blesses the life of a person who has died. It's delivered at a funeral, memorial ceremony, or other gathering of the bereaved. Sometimes more than one person will talk about, or eulogize, the deceased; however, in some religious and secular settings, only one person is given this opportunity.

Eulogies have a long history in Western tradition because they give a voice to our losses. Through talking about them, we begin to heal the grief created by such losses. The word *eulogy*, which comes from Greek, means good words. Sometimes, eulogy is translated as praise or blessing. In this sense, *blessing* means to honor and wish well.

These translations give an idea of what the eulogy is supposed to be, but the speech itself offers an opportunity to say good things about the person who has died, perhaps positive things that we wanted to say to or about a person before death.

In the eulogy, we find ways to praise the essence of the deceased, to look at his or her best qualities

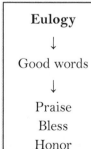

Eulogy
↓
Good words
↓
Praise
Bless
Honor

and the ways he or she lived. We praise someone in a eulogy by speaking well of him or her, admiring virtues and bidding a tender and fond farewell.

Who this person was in terms of character and relationships is much more important than a historical account of what the person did in terms of a job or career. The eulogy gives us a chance to say aloud what was most loveable, human, and special about this person's life. Doing so helps us to build a bridge between life and death. It also forces us to acknowledge that the dead have gone somewhere out of our physical reach. Acknowledging the reality of our loss is essential to healing from it.

As chapter 3 explains, when someone's spiritual beliefs are involved, typically a clergy member offers formal, religion-based blessings for the deceased's spiritual afterlife. However, everyday people like you and me also can offer blessings for both the living and the dead. For the living, we may say something like, "May you have many blessings during this time of grief." For the dead, we may say something like, "May you rest in peace."

We bless by honoring the best of our shared human nature. In a blessing, we examine our feelings for our deceased loved ones and ritually send them from our daily physical lives with best wishes. Blessing a deceased loved one involves active participation in the funeral or memorial ceremony.

A eulogy encourages mourners by naming what we love and will miss about the deceased and urging us to keep that part of him or her in the world. Sometimes, the encouragement is overt:

> *Do what Joanne did and be kind by giving charitably to those less fortunate than you.*

Other times, the encouragement is more covert:

> *Martin's life showed us how to be better people.*

In the first example, we're told specifically what we can do to be like Joanne. In the second example, the actions we could imitate are not named, but we know what they are because our personal relationships with Martin will provide our own examples.

What a Eulogy Isn't

A eulogy isn't an opportunity to air our complaints or hurts. Of course, all of our loved ones have faults, and often we have difficult relationships with them. Just because a eulogy focuses on praise doesn't mean that our loved ones didn't need to change anything in life. The goal of a eulogy isn't to pretend that a person was superhuman or perfect.

As this book shows, it's possible to eulogize a person's positive characteristics while still admitting to human shortcomings. However, a eulogy given at a funeral or memorial service isn't the time or place to list all of the deceased's failings—particularly for those involved in a difficult relationship. As chapter 3 discusses, there are other ways, times, and places to address past hurts and ambiguous feelings.

A eulogy also isn't an exaggerated account of a person's life. When someone dies, it's easy to think of all the wonderful things about the person that we'll miss. But those alone don't create a balanced picture of someone who both has virtues and human flaws. While flaws aren't the focus of a eulogy, it's necessary to acknowledge that the deceased wasn't all good or bad but human in all ways.

On the other hand, it's not about the bowling scores either. A eulogy may use interesting biographical details, but it's focused on the essence of our loved ones—what makes them unique, human, and people of character and value.

A eulogy isn't an obituary or a résumé. Typically, when someone dies, family members contact local newspapers and ask to run an obituary, which is a short notice of a death. It may include information such as a photograph (which is printed in black and white), birth and death dates, names and relationships of family members—particularly those surviving the deceased—career or job information, and where and when the funeral or memorial service will be held.

In short, as this sample obituary written on my father's death shows, the newspaper notice usually isn't terribly personal. Depending on the availability of space and the deceased's impact on the local community, some papers won't be able to print more than a few dozen words, if that. Often, local papers will allow a longer, more detailed obituary than larger regional papers. Sometimes the obituary is written by a family member, and other times it's written by a newspaper employee, depending on the paper's policies.

Sample Obituary

L., George J. C.

Suddenly on December 16, 2001, George J. C., beloved husband of Daryl, devoted father of Beth Ann and her husband Paul H., Michael J. L., Kathryn M. and her husband Murphy W., the late George J. L. and his wife Mary Ann L. Dear brother of Elizabeth W. Also survived by six grandchildren.

Service at Evans Chapel of Memories—Parkville on Thursday at 1 P.M. Interment Gardens of Faith Cemetery. Visiting Wednesday 3 to 5 and 7 to 9 P.M. Memorial donations in George's name may be made to Bereaved Parents USA-Baltimore Metro Area, Inc., P.O. Box 625, Brooklandville, MD 21022-0625.

A eulogy isn't a sermon or a homily. A sermon offers spiritually based messages on Biblical, theological, or religious topics related to particular belief systems, and it usually is delivered by a clergy person (for example, a priest, deacon, pastor, or rabbi).

When a sermon is delivered in connection with a funeral, it's done to draw the audience's attention to the deceased's spiritual faith in God and the afterlife. In other words, it has a sacred purpose. The sermon may mention the deceased with respect to his or her faith and enactment of that faith during life, but it won't have the same purpose as the eulogy of praising, blessing, or honoring the deceased.

While the sermon's focus is sacred in nature, the eulogy is secular, even though they both might talk about elements of spirituality. It's important to understand that eulogies are different from sermons because, as chapter 8 discusses, in certain religions a eulogy can't be a part of the actual funeral ceremony and must be delivered at another time, if at all. If you're concerned about whether a eulogy will be considered appropriate to the kind of funeral or memorial ceremony being planned, consult chapter 8 and the religious presider for the funeral after reading this chapter.

Finally, a eulogy doesn't need to be perfect. One that's written by private citizens like you and me probably won't sound the same as one written for celebrities and public figures such as President Ronald Reagan, Great Britain's Princess Diana, or South African President Nelson Mandela. Funeral speeches for famous people often are written or edited by professional speech writers. In fact, they're often written years before the death and are regularly updated.

That's why famous people's obituaries often are posted to a newspaper or the Internet within hours of their deaths, and it's why their eulogies usually are highly polished speeches.

Most eulogies for private citizens, however, are written by nonprofessional writers, which is appropriate considering that family and friends tend to know the deceased best. Some nonprofessional writers, however, are intimidated by the task of writing a funeral speech for oral delivery. Many people shy from writing the eulogy because it involves putting memories, experiences, and emotions into words at a difficult time. But because a eulogy can assist people in their healing processes, writing and delivering one is an important job.

Where a Eulogy Is Delivered

Typically, a eulogy is delivered at a funeral or other memorial ceremony. These ceremonies can occur at such places as a church or other consecrated or religiously designated building, a funeral home, a private home, a meeting hall or restaurant, or the graveside. The funeral ceremony usually includes an opportunity to view an open or closed casket or an urn in addition to mementos of the deceased.

In a memorial ceremony, the body already has been interred or otherwise situated, and instead there may be photographs or other mementos of the deceased. Of these places, the graveside service is used infrequently for eulogies as there are other rituals relative to burying a casket or urn that may take precedence.

In a consecrated building like a church, the delivery of a eulogy depends greatly on the practices of the religious group using that building for worship. Chapter 8 addresses these practices in more depth. When eulogies are delivered in a funeral home, private home, meeting hall, or restaurant, there may be more flexibility in when and how a eulogy is delivered as these places tend to address the death with rituals that are less oriented toward a particular religion's spirituality. Because the kinds of eulogies described in this book are oriented toward praising the virtuous qualities of the deceased rather than writing biographical sketches, resumes, or exaggerated accounts of the deceased person's accomplishments, it's possible that clergy people of various religions may find them to be acceptable additions to their spiritually based services. In all cases, it's important to check preferences and receive guidance regarding a eulogy with the person who will preside at the ceremony, whether it's a clergy person, funeral director, friend, or family member.

Remembering People

My niece Christina lost her father when she was only thirteen, and she has experienced other deaths since that time. She has strong feelings about using eulogies as sermons:

I attended the funeral of a friend who was killed in a car accident. Although she was spiritual and raised as a Christian, her father completely misrepresented her as a person and turned her eulogy into scare tactics: "Amanda was a devout believer in Jesus, so she's in heaven, and you should do the same."

It was shocking even to the religious Christians present. It caused her friends of other faiths heartache to hear these words. The unfortunate death of a young person is neither an opportunity for people to proselytize nor one to scare survivors straight.

While spirituality is important, I think eulogists need to remember that they're writing about an individual and not about their own convictions.

When a Eulogy Is Written

A eulogy most often is written upon the loved one's death just prior to a funeral or memorial ceremony. This timing means that people write eulogies quickly in only one or two days. When the death is sudden or the bereaved family is from a culture that buries the deceased within 24 – 48 hours, the eulogy may need to be written even more quickly. Time issues can make writing a eulogy especially challenging, which is why chapters 3 and 5 and appendix C are recommended as the primary chapters to read in these cases.

In circumstances where a loved one is in a hospice or hospital setting, there is more time to write the eulogy. People will have time to read this book more slowly. For a variety of reasons, sometimes a eulogy isn't written before the funeral or memorial ceremony. However, it still can be written later as a way to memorialize a loved one. Chapter 8 addresses both pre-writing the eulogy in a hospice or hospital setting, as well as writing the eulogy after the ceremonies are over—even when they've been over for months or years.

What a Eulogy Looks and Sounds Like

Much of this book describes a "traditional" eulogy as a written speech that's delivered by one person at the funeral or memorial ceremony. A traditional eulogy tends to take about six to twelve minutes to deliver. It's difficult to hold everyone's attention any longer than this. Three double-spaced typed pages of 16-point font take about two minutes to read when they're read slowly and with feeling. With these time frames and font sizes in mind, a finished eulogy may be about nine to eighteen pages long. Within these boundaries, the eulogy praises the deceased person with illustrations of virtues and noble actions. Even if praise is not easy for any set of reasons, the eulogy still can bless and honor the deceased.

This example of my brother George's eulogy shows an approximately twelve minute speech that was written to praise his generosity, sense of adventure, and enthusiasm for life.

Eulogy for George J. L.

We're gathered here today to mourn the death and celebrate the life of George L., beloved husband, father, son, brother, and friend. A week ago, had you asked any of us what we would be doing on this summer afternoon, none of us would have guessed that we would be attending George's funeral.

I could stand here and tell you of George's accomplishments—and they were many: he was an Eagle Scout, a respected nuclear/electrical engineer and consultant, a world traveler who visited such foreign countries as Suriname, Russia, the Ukraine, Germany, France, Canada, the islands of the Bahamas, and Dundalk. I could tell you that he was a skilled pilot, a ski-buff, a photographer, and a budding poet. I could tell you that he played flag football and mastered the dulcimer and told stories that made us laugh and cry. I could tell you that he was a devoted husband to Mary Ann and a doting, if occasionally impatient, father to George, Virginia, and Christina—nothing was impossible when it came to his children. I could tell you that he was a devout Christian, who took seriously his call to reach out to his parents, to his brother and sisters, to his nephews and niece, and to his friends, who always could call on him for help, anytime, day or night. But you know all that. And so, given George's inherent goodness and love of life, we might wonder how it's that he is gone from us today, leaving us to mourn his untimely death and to find the strength to celebrate his life.

But by looking at the rich fullness of George's life, we might take comfort in knowing that he lived at least *two lifetimes* in his short 44 years—and he lived those years both in wonder at God's great gifts and with the grace to allow us to share in his mistakes and personal growth. For George, far from perfect, was a human being who relished his own growth and who found humor and encouragement in our development, as well. He was a man of deep introspection and he never was afraid to let us share in his errors, knowing perhaps that we would benefit from the laughter that he provided and the lessons that he learned. And George did make us laugh. He did this with physical, as well as verbal, humor.

When George was in his early teens, he cajoled his sister Beth to climb a small mountain with him in Bloomsburg, Pennsylvania. The idea was to take his hosts' toboggan and ride it down the mountain as fast as it could go; to do that, he needed more weight and so his sister was called upon to do her duty. Up they trudged for hours in thigh-deep snow. At the top, they got on the toboggan, George in front to steer and Beth in back as ballast. They started down the mountain side at breathtaking speed. What happened next was a mystery to them both. A tree jumped out in front, George dove off the toboggan, and the sled and Beth struck the tree. He'd forgotten to tell her to jump! The toboggan was broken, Beth was badly bruised and momentarily unconscious, and once he had overcome his initial fear that she was dead, George rose to the occasion—solemnly pulling the broken and twisted toboggan down the mountain while Beth limped behind. And he was elated. For he had discovered the thrill of speed, and with that discovery, he both delighted and scared us over the years.

At sixteen, he got his driver's license and a 1950s vintage Saab sedan. He drove that Saab up and down Harford Road, cruising the streets, pretending to be Harrison Ford in *American Graffiti*. Only the boldest of his friends failed to feel some rush of anxious excitement at the speeds with which he would drive. Later, as a new husband, he took some friends to Herring Run Park, intending to show them how safe it was to sled down these hills—instead, he fell and fractured his own hand. Safe? Who cared when George was demonstrating the lay of the land? Once, when skiing, he hit a mogul, broke half a ski, and continued down the mountain on one ski with the broken ski lifted high, singing the Olympics theme song. A young girl turned to her mother and said, "Look, Mom, a stunt skier!" Not content to confine his skiing stunts to his own life, George once talked his soon-to-be brother-in-law Murphy, a very novice skier, into skiing down a double black diamond slope. When they finally made it down the hill nearly 2 hours later, his sister Kathy sighed with relief, knowing that George had showed his approval of her future husband by bringing him back safely.

Yes, George made us laugh, and not just with his ever growing desire for speed and the thrills of mastering gravity. When he broke his first window at age four, his mother was elated; she knew she had a real boy who was mischievous and daring. When he played varsity football, he was the only team member to come off the field with a jersey as clean as when he had gone onto the field; yet, his teammates always knew that he'd played his heart out. One time, as a new homeowner, he went onto his roof to fix the shingles and off he fell, later telling the story and giggling like a teenager. Another time, he took his son George hunting and pulled the trigger of his rifle to check the safety, shooting a hole into the floor of his VW Vanagon. Young George held his hands over his ears and cried out: "Daddy! Don't do that again! That hurt my ears!" To celebrate his ridiculous mistake, George mounted deer antlers to the van's hood and claimed it as his first "kill" of the season. Mishaps that showed his humanness followed George like ants to a picnic. At his first job as a garage mechanic, he put his finger into a battery case to see whether the battery fluid was there—and burned himself with the acidic liquid. He drove his Vanagon until it died, once using a rope as an accelerator. When that car finally died a fiery death, he left a simple phone message for Mary Ann: "Van burned up. I'm ok. Talk to you later." We can all see her face as she shook her head in wonder and exasperation. George once bought a Carmen Ghia for $1,000; it had no wheels and looked like it never would see the road again. After a year of loving care and slavishly hard work, George had it shiny and road-worthy again. He sold it for a whopping $1,000 and felt satisfied.

So that was George. But this also was George:

- When he married Mary Ann, during the first dance with his bride, he swept her off her feet and ran through the door with her, leaving no questions as to his devotion to his new wife. How many of us would like to be able to show our love so unselfconsciously? On July 12, he and his bride celebrated 20 years of marriage and found it beautiful, ready for 20 more.

- Every year, George took his son and invited his nephews and their fathers to the Brotherhood of the Jungle Cock's Father and Boy fishing camp; he took young George on a week-long Boy Scout canoeing trip. Nothing was more important than helping young boys to become men.

- George took his daughter Virginia and her friends skiing. The friends, who vowed they hated skiing, worked with George until they mastered the beginner slopes and found themselves in love with a new sport. Ever the brave soul, George recently took Virginia and 4 teenage friends to the beach—they had a 4 wonderful days.

- George took special care with Christina, too, who we all know as Boop. Although she was the third child, she was far from last in his heart. Every Tuesday morning before French class, he took Boop out to breakfast and before bed each night, she'd say, "I know what you're gonna say," to which he always replied, "Have a good day in school tomorrow."

- George was always ready to come when his parents needed him; he never pulled out his calendar to make a date—he just looked at his watch and said, "What time?" For his mother-in-law, Geraldine, there always was a place in his home and in his heart.

- He helped his sister Beth to find the courage to leave a devastating job situation, supporting her sense of self value. George helped his brother Mike enter manhood by teaching him not only the practical skills that he would need, but by demonstrating the values of physical sacrifice and mental determination, and by passing on the love and wisdom of Bruce Springsteen. Whenever Kathy needed a brother's ear or someone to set her straight, she knew she could call on George.

- And he was there for friends and community, too. George's football and high school buddies always knew he would come to the annual flag football get-together. Wherever he went, for work or for pleasure, he picked up a phone and kept in contact with friends, cousins, other relatives, and co-workers. If someone he knew had an emergency or a tragedy or a blessing, George was there—time or cost not a factor.

In fact, George was an incredibly extroverted person, one who actually gained energy when he was around other people and one who was drained by being alone. And so, when his Saturday chore was to clean the garage, he did it talking on the phone or calling on his friends just to come and be with him while he worked. And friends came. Why not? George would have been there for them and he was always good for a laugh and a story.

Each one of us here today knows these and other stories that tell of George's life. Most of us also know that George bravely conquered alcoholism and has been sober for ten years. He used his relationship with God and with other people to strengthen his resolve when the going got tough. Maybe he encouraged you to kick your own harmful habit. If so, you have special reason to be grateful for this short-lived but graceful man's influence.

Let me talk about one more thing before closing this most difficult eulogy. George loved to fly. He was a good pilot and had more than 20 years' experience. Both of his parents, his children and wife, numerous friends, and both of his nephews and his niece had flown with him. Some of the earliest flight training he provided was to "fly" the family babies on the palm of his hand—before they could even sit up on their own. He was going to teach his sister Beth to fly. And, even with a bumpy and broken landing last Fourth of July, Mary Ann trusted his skill and judgment and supported his new career choice—to be a flight instructor.

Just this past month, George left his position at *PECO* to start his own company: *Check Six Flight Experiences*. To make emotional space for his new ultra-light glider that he was going to use as a teaching plane, he made a charitable donation of the unfinished airplane that he was building. Then, in the beginning of this month, he flew his new plane from Illinois. Here are his words from a draft of an article that he wrote just last week about that trip: "My first landing attempt downwind was high and fast so I executed a go-around. My second attempt was dead-on. What a thrill! After I shut down the engine, my wife and daughter ran over to greet me. I did it! This was my first long cross-country in over five years and my first in an ultra-light. And while I flew the plane alone, I made the trip with all those who helped me plan, prepare, supply equipment, and think about and pray for me. Thank you all for your support."

And so, as we mourn George and celebrate his life, let us not be angry with him for his love of speed and his love of flying, for those loves combined to make him who he was. Let us say, along with him, *"Oh, I have slipped the surly bonds of earth, And danced the skies on laughter silvered wings."* George, when you touch the face of God, please say hello to Him for us.

From a less traditional perspective, a eulogy can take more contemporary forms that chapter 8 discusses. Beyond an oral speech delivered by one person, it might be delivered as a multi-vocal collaboration where two or more people speak different parts of the eulogy. Or, it can be the product of two or more people who each have their own eulogies to give. The eulogy can be delivered as letter to the deceased or even as a letter from the deceased to the gathered mourners. Because medical and hospice professionals often encourage dying people and their families to talk about what is happening, we may hear letters from the deceased who knew they were dying and who wanted to send their own words of comfort to mourners. The Internet also offers new ways to read, hear, and interact with eulogies as they can be presented through "YouTube" videos. Mourners can respond with their own videos or written comments. The contemporary eulogy can be more visual than oral in that many funeral and memorial ceremonies include photo and video montages of the deceased person's life. Chapter 8 talks more about these kinds of media.

Contemporary Eulogies
⚘ Two or more people delivering the eulogy
⚘ Multiple attendees sharing memories
⚘ A letter to or from the deceased
⚘ Internet-based "YouTube" videos with written or video responses by mourners
⚘ Photo and video montages
⚘ Other creative possibilities

Even with the rising popularity of newer eulogy forms, the good words of a traditional eulogy will always have their place and value. By learning about the traditional eulogy, it will be easier to plan and develop more contemporary ways of eulogizing—of saying "good words"—that reflect your grief and touch the hearts of fellow mourners.

Chapter 2

Why Should I Write a Eulogy?

How a Eulogy Helps Us

Grief is an internalized response to death. A eulogy externalizes grief by giving it a voice through words. It both memorializes the deceased and builds up the grieving community by helping mourners make good use of the funeral or memorial ceremony's public space.

The ritual of a eulogy provides a social space for mourning. By *speaking about the deceased* to the gathered mourners, the eulogist *speaks for the bereaved*—naming what people admired about the deceased, what they will miss about him or her, and how the deceased has influenced the world. Because of this important task of speaking for the bereaved, the eulogy writer often is one of the bereaved family members or has consulted them in writing the eulogy. When it's well written and delivered, the eulogy brings the family and community together and provides comfort through the shared experience of mourning. As such, a eulogy both reinforces and broadens the community's view of the deceased.

My mother calls the anniversary of someone's death the "angel date." On the eve of my brother's eight-year angel date, she shared that she has no memory of standing at George's graveside. She knows she was there, but cannot remember any of that ceremony.

Eulogies offer other benefits to those who hear them (and even to those who later read the eulogy silently). The eulogist uses the funeral speech to articulate thoughts and feelings for the bereaved at a particularly inarticulate time. The immediate family may be in a state of shock—even for an expected death of a terminally ill loved one. In that state, family members may greet people and appear to be functional although they later may say that they don't remember much of the funeral. Stunned and dazed family members often need the eulogist to say the words they can't articulate at this painful time.

Hearing or reading a eulogy provides mourners with other words, new words, good words that suggest a wide variety of ways to express the loss. The eulogy enables verbal and emotional expressions of grief, and even physical expressions like crying, hugging, holding hands, leaning forward, or rocking one's body. These physical expressions can help the bereaved communicate their grief.

Like the act of viewing a body (or an urn or a closed casket), the eulogy provides a reality check. It clearly states that, *yes, this person is indeed dead and, yes, the mourning has begun officially.* In a way, the eulogist becomes a teacher who leads the mourning community by describing his or her grief. The eulogist's words invite others to reflect on their own grief and to participate in a more communal, shared experience of mourning. As part of the funeral ceremony, the eulogy provides another meaningful time, place, and method for reflecting on the loss of a beloved person. Often, it includes opportunities for other people to speak informally about, and contemplate on, their loss.

Examples of Deceased's Values Matching Those of the Community

- If the deceased was a devout Christian and has a Christian funeral ceremony, then the eulogy likely will highlight some of the Christian virtues that the gathered mourners will understand and appreciate.
- If the deceased was a local politician who never expressed a particular spirituality, the eulogy probably will highlight the common life values that the mourners likely hold—for example: integrity, honesty, and giving of self to others.

On a broader social level, the eulogy actually instills

and reinforces values by teaching gathered mourners about their society and cultural ideals and ethics. Through the selected details of the deceased person's life, the eulogy writer illustrates those virtues, attitudes, and actions that the community expects, values, and praises as evidence of a life well lived. The eulogy shows how the deceased met these values in his or her lifetime. Because the mourners cared about or admired the deceased, the values that the eulogy illustrates likely would match the mourners' values. If their values match, the eulogy reinforces them. If their values don't match, the eulogy gives the mourners a chance to learn about them. However, particularly in a secular setting, it's a good rule of thumb to keep faith-based assessments general unless the deceased openly shared his or her beliefs with others. To press one's own spirituality on a heterogeneous audience can stunt others' grieving processes.

Another way a eulogy can help us is in healing regretful and angry feelings about the nature or cause of the deceased's death.

Eulogy for Healing Grievances

The Gettysburg Address
Abraham Lincoln
November 19, 1863

Four score and seven years ago our fathers brought forth on this continent, a new nation, conceived in Liberty, and dedicated to the proposition that all men are created equal.

Now we are engaged in a great civil war, testing whether that nation, or any nation so conceived and so dedicated, can long endure. We are met on a great battle-field of that war. We have come to dedicate a portion of that field, as a final resting place for those who here gave their lives that that nation might live. It is altogether fitting and proper that we should do this.

But, in a larger sense, we cannot dedicate—we cannot consecrate—we cannot hallow— this ground. The brave men, living and dead, who struggled here, have consecrated it, far above our poor power to add or detract. The world will little note, nor long remember what we say here, but it can never forget what they did here. It is for us the living, rather, to be dedicated here to the unfinished work which they who fought here have thus far so nobly advanced. It is rather for us to be here dedicated to the great task remaining before us—that from these honored dead we take increased devotion to that cause for which they gave the last full measure of devotion—that we here highly resolve that these dead shall not have died in vain—that this nation, under God, shall have a new birth of freedom—and that government of the people, by the people, for the people, shall not perish from the earth.

The *Gettysburg Address*, one of America's shortest and most famous funeral speeches, was written by President Abraham Lincoln to memorialize the soldiers who died at the Gettysburg Battlefield during the last days of the Civil War. In a spirit of shared mourning for the thousands of dead soldiers and their bereaved families and friends, he equally praised and lamented soldiers from both the North and the South. Lincoln's words began the difficult process of uniting the country while simultaneously supporting the bereaved citizens on both sides. He focused beyond the terrible hurts of the Civil War and led his listeners (and later those who read the short address) to begin to understand both southern and northern states as essential to the largest community—the United States.

In a similar way, the eulogy for my brother was designed to help those who might express their pain through anger or blame at George for dying while flying. How could his family and friends not feel some kind of anger that *if only* he hadn't decided to fly (that day, or ever, or in an ultra-light plane), he would still be alive? It was an especially difficult situation because no one knew then who had control of the plane at the time it crashed. It could have been my brother or it could have been his student, who was an experienced pilot of other types of aircraft. It wasn't my brother's plane, but he was the instructor. Who or what was at fault? It took years and a court case against the manufacturer of the plane's engine to discover with any degree of certainty that a faulty engine was the primary cause. And that, of course, was long after the funeral ceremony.

It was essential in writing the eulogy to deal directly with George's decision to fly and to teach in an ultra-light aircraft. That's why the last three paragraphs in the eulogy were dedicated to his love for flying, his family's acceptance and support of it, and his experience and desire to continue developing his skills (see chapter 1). The words were deliberately planned to remind people that George's death was an accident that could have happened at any time or place. In this way, the eulogy helped the mourners grieve without the burden of "if only" wishes that often lead to blame. Such blame eventually could interfere with their healing and peace around his tragic death.

Grief and Mourning

The eulogy is one part of the healing process that the bereaved need. Usually, it's delivered during a funeral or memorial ceremony, which provides the time and a formal place to begin mourning a person who has died. Such ceremonies are rare opportunities for people to come together in support of one another. They help people experience the healing nature of rituals that support the bereaved in beginning their mourning.

It's helpful here to understand a crucial difference between the concepts of "grief" and "mourning." Grief tends to hit us like a punch in the gut as soon as we hear of a loved one's death—or as soon as the shock that cushions us wears off. Mourning, on the other hand, isn't as automatic. One way to look at these concepts is that *grief is an internalized, involuntary process* and *mourning is an externalized, voluntary process that actually helps to heal and soften grief.*

Grief is:

- Internalized
- Involuntary
- Experienced in emotional, spiritual, and physical ways

Mourning is:

- Externalized
- Voluntary
- Conveyed in actions that help to heal the emotional, spiritual, and physical self

When we're bereaved, we experience sadness on many levels—emotional, spiritual, and physical. According to Dr. Alan Wolfelt, who is a prominent counselor and author about grief, grief is a feeling or set of emotions that we experience as a result of the loss of a loved one.[1] We may even experience these feelings on hearing about the death of someone we know but aren't closely connected to—like a co-worker or a friend's parent.

Emotionally, we might experience feelings like:

- Sadness
- Pain
- Anger
- Fear
- Emptiness
- Confusion
- Loneliness

Spiritually, we may experience:

- A sense of anger or distance from God
- Doubt about our previously held beliefs
- An increased intensity of beliefs

Physically, we might experience grief symptoms such as:

- Tears
- Insomnia
- Sleepiness
- Increase or decrease in appetite
- Pain in various parts of the body
- Restlessness
- Lack of energy
- Anxiety

---

[1] There are many helpful books for those who are grieving a loved one. Two of these are my own *More Good Words: Practical Activities for Mourning* (Bloomington, IN: WestBow Press, 2014) and Alan Wolfelt's *Understanding Your Grief: Ten Essential Touchstones for Finding Hope and Healing Your Heart* (Ft. Collins, CO: Companion Press, 2004).

Grief can underlie these and many more emotional, spiritual, and physical symptoms. Dr. Wolfelt teaches that mourning, on the other hand, is action-based. Rather than merely feeling grief, *mourning is what we do with grief.* If we only feel grief and never do anything with it, it's possible that we'll become emotionally, spiritually, or physically sick. Without the mourning process, it may take longer to return to some state of emotional, spiritual, or physical moderation and balance.

When we mourn, we give voice to the feelings of grief. For example, crying, wailing, and keening (that is, howling, often accompanied by physical gestures like rocking back and forth) are ways that vocalize the pain of grief. Giving voice to grief also happens with our hands—sewing a memorial quilt, planting a tree, or cooking a beloved's favorite meal. *More Good Words: Practical Activities for Mourning* details and illustrates these and other ways to actively mourn our loved ones.

As noted above, a funeral or memorial ceremony provides a way to express grief and to facilitate the mourning process. While grief is triggered by the immediate loss of the deceased person's physical presence, this loss also reminds us of our own mortality. When someone we know dies, we have the opportunity to confront the reality of death on multiple levels. Each opportunity is unique to the person who is grieving and is influenced by the life of the one who has died.

Looking at Death in America

Confronting the reality of death is an important concept to explore. Contemporary American society has been called a "culture of death" in that we're bombarded with the spectacle of sensationalized death to the point that many people have become numb to it. We see bloody and meaningless death in the media daily—on television programs, in movies, and through televised, newspaper, and Internet-based news stories. We hear powerful tales of death in popular songs. As a country, we have war casualties. We even "play" with death in actively visual, audible ways through video, computer, and other games.

Beth L. Hewett, Ph.D.

And yet, we experience this culture of death as spectators. We lack recognition, understanding, and respect for the toll that death takes on us as bereaved human beings. In fact, our society avoids both grief and mourning. In the grief support groups, seminars, and retreats that I've facilitated, I've heard sad tales of folks who have lost friends and even their jobs because, according to others, they haven't been able to shake their grief soon enough to be considered functional. People want the bereaved to "move on" because grief makes them uncomfortable. In terms of relationships, sometimes friends are so uneasy with grief that they stop coming around after a few weeks. Although they probably still care a lot about their bereaved friends, they simply don't know how to help or what to say. At work, many employers offer workers only three to five paid days off to attend a funeral and get themselves back into action.

Bereaved people need time to process the loss and to experience their grief fully. Even though our culture is obsessed with death, it doesn't adequately support or provide time to process that death. On television shows, for example, a much-loved character might die in a shocking scene. In the next episode, that character may be mentioned in passing

Funeral and Memorial Ceremonies:

- Give us a chance to vocalize our grief
- Help us to begin mourning
- Provide an opportunity to confront the reality of the loss
- Encourage the bereaved through the support of other mourners
- Build a community of shared mourners
- Externalize the grief through public mourning like crying, holding each other, and reflecting with others about the deceased

and there may be a few displays of sadness (and often a desire for revenge), but rarely are the devastating feelings of grief acted out and developed over time. Soon, the lost character is all but forgotten, replaced by the idiosyncrasies of a new character.

In real life, the bereaved often are told that they should be "over it" mere months after a significant loss. Those around the bereaved may minimize the loss, sometimes trying to soothe their own discomfort about death with phrases like "he's better off now" and "at least she died quickly." Thus, the bereaved are isolated by messages that they're too focused on their grief just when they most need the support and understanding of others.

My point is that the ritual of a funeral or memorial ceremony is critical to acknowledging the world-shattering nature of a beloved one's death. Yet all too frequently, the entire funeral or memorial ritual is skipped as a way of not "dwelling" on the loss or in the mistaken belief that it is an outdated activity and unnecessary expense. In fact, the shared experience of a community ceremony serves to make us aware of the mutual and inevitable nature of death helping us confront our own mortality and show compassion for the bereaved.

Because humans are social beings, we need opportunities to share our grief and to mourn together. The funeral or memorial ceremony enables us to come together in a shared social setting of mourning.

> **The Eulogy Can:**
>
> * Help the bereaved to process their loss and to experience grief in healthy ways
> * Put into words what the bereaved loved most about the deceased
> * Encourage a communal sharing of the grief
> * Support the bereaved, especially the family, as they awaken from the shock of the death
> * Instill and reinforce shared community values
> * Directly and sensitively address difficult circumstances to support healing

At the ceremony, we form a temporary community of mourners whose very presence serves as an expression of our common grief and of our mutual support for the bereaved. Funeral rituals like the eulogy engage the mourning process to externalize the individual's grief and share it publicly with others.

At a funeral or memorial ceremony, people strengthen one another by recalling the deceased in positive ways that support the bereaved and help them face their loss and to begin the hard work of mourning. Family, friends, and co-workers bear witness to the deceased person's life, as well as to the continuing life of those who survive him or her. That's why there's so much crying, talking, and laughing that goes on at these ceremonies. They're rarely silent affairs; nor should they be silent. It's by vocalizing that we externalize grief and enable mourning to begin. The eulogy is one of the most important vocalizations that we have in the funeral or memorial ceremony.

Chapter 3

What Good Words Do I Say?

If you only have time to read one chapter of this book, this is the one to read! Use this chapter with the "Eulogy Writing Guide" in appendix C at the back of the book.

Figuring Out What to Write

Now that you know what a eulogy is and why it's important to write one, you're probably wondering what to write. You may ask, *"What will I say to show everyone how special my mother was?"* or *"How can I express the beauty that was my little boy?"* or *"How can I write a eulogy when we've been fighting for all these years?"* Those are tough questions. It can be hard to figure out what to write about a family member, friend, or co-worker. The goal is to pay tribute to this person, but most bereaved people are under tremendous time pressure and emotional stress. Few people can do their best writing under those conditions.

That's why this chapter provides two specific ways to approach good words for the deceased. The first way is to write a traditional eulogy, which works especially well when it's easy to find things to praise in the deceased's character and life. The second way is appropriate when the eulogist's (or others') relationship to the deceased is strained or when there are difficult circumstances surrounding the death. In such cases, rather than write a traditional eulogy, it's possible to offer good words by honoring the human nature of the deceased, which is a way of blessing him or her. This chapter first will address how to find good words for the traditional eulogy. The second half of the chapter will focus on how to develop an appropriate blessing.

Finding Good Words for the Traditional Eulogy

Step 1: Talk with Family Members

Although you might at first feel alone as the writer, writing a eulogy is an extremely collaborative process. That's why the first and most important step in the eulogy writing process is to talk with those people who knew the deceased the best. Family members and close friends usually have memories of their loved ones that they'd like to share. They also have different insights and perspectives about the deceased. While they might not be the best people to write the eulogy, they are crucial to providing its basic content. Without their input—even if you're also a family member—you risk offending or alienating someone for whom this funeral or memorial ceremony is necessary.

One example of needing input occurred when I was writing my father's eulogy. My surviving younger brother wanted to offer some thoughts, and he read my draft. One of the key anecdotes about my father (who also was named George) had to do with his loss of fingers as an adolescent. My brother pointed out that some of the details I wanted to provide about my father's accident were inappropriate to include because he understood that discussing the circumstances deeply upset our father. I had wanted to use Dad's limited use of that hand to illustrate how he used this loss positively in his life. Together, my brother and I worked out that the accident itself was unimportant to share, while how it changed our father's life was critical. Our work together helped to ensure that the eulogy didn't have details that would have upset my family.

Passage from My Father's Eulogy Illustrating How to Acknowledge the Impact of a Situation without Giving Unnecessary Details

Many of you know that George lost three fingers to an adolescent injury, but most of you probably don't know how profoundly the accident influenced his life. With two complete hands, George would have fought for his country in Korea, a lost opportunity that always saddened him. So, instead, as an adult, George served his community as Cub Master, sports booster, and visionary for Parkville's revitalization. Professionally, George may have entered any one of several hands-on fields, such as contracting. But the loss of his fingers, though physically and psychically painful, led him to use his analytical mind. He put his love of building into drafting and, later, into engineering.

Step 2: Gently Elicit Information from Family Members

What else can family members and close friends tell you about the deceased? There are at least three kinds of information that you should try to get:

1. Factual details

2. Biographical stories

3. Character qualities

Factual Details

The first kind of information is personal details or the basic facts of one's life. Many of these facts actually are used in an obituary, as chapter 1 shows. You'll want the person's legal name and whether a middle name or nickname should be used in the eulogy. Other such details include:

- Dates of birth and death (hence, age)
- Date/s of marriage/s (if he or she currently has a spouse and children)
- Names and number of children or siblings, if any

- Level of education and the name of the school/s
- Current or past career/s (including the company name if co-workers may attend the services)
- Any other details that the family wants to provide (here is where you may learn that the deceased had a sibling who died at birth, for example)

Using the space provided in appendix C's "Eulogy Writer's Guide" at the back of the book, record some of the factual details about the deceased that bereaved family and friends might want in the eulogy.

It's easy to make the mistake of using only factual details in a eulogy. At their worst, such details lead to a kind of generic résumé of the deceased's life—or even a slightly longer version of the obituary. You don't need to include every date or person in the deceased person's life. But by starting your research with a fact list, you'll be able to figure out what's necessary to include as you move into the second kind of information—biographical stories.

Biographical Stories

Biographical stories include the family and friends' memories and favorite anecdotes about the deceased. Here, you may want to ask each person for a story about the loved one. You can gently prime the pump by asking such questions as:

- What is your favorite memory of your daddy?
- When you saw your mom or talked to her on the phone, was there something you could always count on her to say or do?
- What did you love best about your little brother?
- Your sister had six children and they all seemed so happy with her. Did she ever tell you how she managed to raise them so well?
- I know you only got to see your cousin in the summertime at the farm. What did you like best about seeing her for the first time each year?

✻ What would Sam's college friends say about him as a fraternity brother?

These kinds of questions lead family members to tell stories that you can record on paper (or by voice recorder, if desired). At the same time, they allow the bereaved to talk about their loved one in positive ways. If, by chance, you ask a question that leads to an unhappy memory, you can help the bereaved person by:

✻ Listening thoughtfully;
✻ Assuring them that you won't share this unhappiness in the eulogy; and
✻ Explaining that you understand that both good and bad memories come up with a loved one's death.

Then, perhaps, you can prompt another, more positive memory for the eulogy.

This next example shows a few lines from the eulogy written for Herb. Neither his daughter nor any of her close family was asked for input into the eulogy, which consequently never said anything more personal or emotionally satisfying than the segment shown here. In fact, rather than bringing the mourners together and comforting them, this eulogy deeply depressed some family members who listened hard to find the essence of their beloved father and grandfather in the words.

Without the Input of Family and Friends, Herb's Original Eulogy Lacked Heartfelt Sentiments and Personal Anecdotes

None of us can adequately speak for him. His achievements and accomplishments are monumental. They speak for him!!!

In the early years of his career, he became a teaching professor at college, Vanderbilt. It was soon discovered that he was an extremely gifted person. His brilliance and intellect rapidly surfaced. Soon he was recognized as a born leader and an able administrator.

He knew the game of life with its frustrations, and accepted its challenges. His integrity and values were of the highest.

When he eventually was advanced to a very high medical administrative position, he accepted his responsibilities unerringly. He headed a very large staff—all medical experts—yet, somehow he always managed to show humility, compassion, fairness, and decency.

While this excerpt shows high praise of Herb, what is lacking is a sense of Herb as a person—the human essence of Herb that made him a memorable person, besides being a good scientist and colleague. And, although a lot of adjectives were used to describe Herb (for example, "monumental," "able administrator," and "unerringly"), we don't know why those words were applied to him and how they were especially fitting. Such adjectives and nouns like "brilliance" and "intellect" make Herb sound almost too good to be real.

A story from an old co-worker, if available, would have helped here as would input from other family members. A personal reminiscence of his relationship with his wife would have been a good illustration, for example. In effect, rather than "showing" something about Herb, the original eulogy "told" about him. The telling made Herb seem somehow stiff and two-dimensional. With the addition of some anecdotes, the revised lines more strongly praise Herb with good words (for the complete revised eulogy, see appendix A).

Revised Eulogy for Herb with Input from Family and Friends

Determined to raise his children as intellectually and physically adventurous people, Herb first taught himself the skills that he would then teach Bob and Susan. Bob wanted to learn to target shoot, so Herb learned skeet shooting first. Susan wanted to travel, so they took trips each summer and visited art museums on the weekend. They studied maps and read books about their destinations in order to make the most of their travels. In the style of a true Renaissance man, Herb demonstrated his deep love of science through his avid interaction with nature. Each year, he took his children to wilderness areas in Minnesota and surrounding states. They camped, fished, hiked, swam, canoed, boated, and water-skied. They canoed from Minnesota to the state's boundary waters. They did things the hard way so that Herb could teach Bob and Susan the strength of character they would need as adults. When they camped, they carried their own equipment on their backs, and when they canoed, they portaged their own canoes.

Just like the factual details, not every biographical memory needs to go into a eulogy. But it's helpful to have something representative to tell in relation to key family members, friends, and co-workers who will be at the services. That's because the funeral and memorial services exist both to spiritually bless and memorialize the deceased and to support and assist the living. It's human nature that people who attend a loved one's funeral or memorial service also are thinking about their own relationships with the deceased. They appreciate hearing that their interactions are valued enough to be remembered in the eulogy. In fact, as I discuss in chapter 7, using someone's exact words really can personalize the eulogy and help them see the good words as reflecting their own relationship with the deceased.

Use the space provided in the appendix C "Eulogy Writing Guide" to record some of the biographical stories that you learn from the family and friends of the deceased.

Although you don't need to make any decisions yet about which ones to include in the eulogy, you might place a check by those anecdotes you think particularly illustrate the deceased.

The third kind of information that you'll consider, that of character qualities, will help you to make your decisions.

Character Qualities

Although biographical details like a love for golf or reading or dog breeding can illustrate a person's interests, a eulogy is most memorable when it explores one's life in terms of its deeper value and importance to those around him or her. Now that you have some factual and biographical details about the deceased, it's time to consider what qualities or characteristics people most admire about him or her. This third kind of information will help you to choose which facts or biographical details you'll include. It also will help you to develop a primary theme—or story—for the eulogy. For example, the primary theme for my brother's eulogy is a love of adventure and speed. The primary theme in Ruth's eulogy (see appendix A) is how the *Bible's* "Book of Wisdom," or "Proverbs," guided her life.

The virtues and noble activities that have guided this person's life will also guide and shape the eulogy. These qualities are essential to understanding the most endearing characteristics of people. And, these qualities are the most enduring ones that people will remember years from now about your loved one.

Virtues are character qualities that demonstrate moral goodness or righteousness. Although none of us has lived a perfect life, most of us have acquired one or more of these virtues:

- Justice
- Courage
- Self-control
- Generosity
- Fairness
- Gentleness
- Integrity
- Patience
- Passion
- Respect
- Commitment
- Dependability
- Selflessness
- Thoughtfulness
- Life-based wisdom
- Knowledge-based wisdom

Noble activities are actions that we recognize as being good for family, friends, local community, or greater society. These are the actions that matter beyond us as individuals. For example, a teenager who spends part of her summer working for Habitat for the Homeless has engaged in a noble activity. Noble activities include:

- Actions that help others
- Honorable deeds
- Unselfish behavior
- Acts of self-sacrifice, justice, and kindness
- Acts that bring credit to oneself or one's family in the eyes of the community and greater society[2]

When used as a method of "discovering" what to say about the deceased, these virtues and noble activities become tools for exploring the person's life. They provide unique personal qualities and past actions to talk about in the eulogy. How do virtues and noble activities help to find ideas and focus the speech?

Just like it's helpful to ask family members questions about factual and biographical details, it's also helpful to ask questions about virtues and noble actions. The goal isn't to have someone answer them with "yes" or "no." The goal is to stimulate people's memories about the deceased's best qualities when they're not necessarily thinking in terms of the big picture.

Let's use the virtue of *courage* as an example. Courage is much more than the narrow belief that any activity that puts a person in danger leads to being a "hero," although this certainly is one valid meaning of courage. Let's look at the example below.

A husband, who also is a father, has died unexpectedly. He will be greatly missed. How did his life exhibit the virtue of courage?

At the personal level: Did this man change his own life by prevailing over difficult childhood adversities—like losing a parent, or living in poverty, or attending many different schools, or putting himself

---

[2] Some of these virtues and noble activities are taken from Aristotle's *The Art of Rhetoric*.

through college? Did he fight a disease, battle with a mental disorder, or otherwise "take on" his own well-being, improving it somehow? Did he learn or teach any important lessons about acting bravely in the face of adversity?

At the family level: Did he support his wife through her own struggles, choosing to stay with her when others might have left? Did he challenge authorities on the basis of his family's survival and wellbeing? Did he support his children even when doing so would seem unlikely or difficult, such as standing by a child who was in trouble with the law? Did he walk side-by-side with a child who struggled with drug addiction? Did he stand up for the rights of an elderly parent who needed an advocate?

At the community level: Did he engage in courageous acts of civil obedience, where there was danger present in preserving or following the law? Did he help to change a bad policy or create a good one when doing so might endanger himself or his family's wellbeing or reputation? Was he injured or killed in the "line of duty"—acts that illustrate the most common perception of courage?

At the societal level: Was he a popular, famous, elected, or otherwise well-known individual that people could emulate for his courage? Was he unknown to others—not "born for fame"— but did he nonetheless earn fame because of an act of courage? For example, was he the first of his culture or ethnicity to face a particular situation or to overcome a serious challenge? Was he a professional like a photographer who captured images that changed the world's view of poverty or crime or genocide?

How do these questions about courage lead to material for a eulogy? In the case of a famous person, the answer might seem simple—celebrity makes for many things to say. There were a variety of good things said about President Ronald Reagan, Britain's Princess Diana, and South Africa's President Nelson Mandela that indicated some degree of courage. Of course, not everyone gets to be a country's leader or a celebrity princess, but it helps to remember that these titles by themselves do not necessarily reveal courage.

For example, Christopher Reeve was one celebrity who was not particularly "courageous" at the height of his early fame as an actor. When he acted in the *Superman* movies of the 1980s, his courage was not celebrated as much as his good looks and personal charm. His paralysis from a horse riding accident wasn't what made him courageous, either—even though it temporarily increased his fame. Instead, the acts that most demonstrated his courage were Reeve's nine-year quest for a good life as a paraplegic, his efforts to be a loving husband and father and to find meaning in personal tragedy, and his hard work to support advances in medical science's understanding of spinal injuries. At the most basic level, however, Reeve's courage literally enabled him to breathe in and breathe out. Sometimes, it's simply at that most basic level that a person reveals courage worthy of our praise and admiration.

Christopher Reeves

Fame → Superman→ charm → handsome → horse riding accident → paraplegic

Courage → living a good life as paraplegic:

- Loving husband and father
- Finding meaning in personal tragedy
- Supporting advances in spinal injury science
- Breathing in and out—minute by minute for nine years

In the case of an everyday husband and father, as in this example, did he exhibit courage and, if so, what did that courage look like to others?

Perhaps the deceased husband and father suffered a childhood injury, losing a limb to an accident that could have crippled his view of himself and his approach to life; but by surmounting that obstacle, such that others hardly noticed what he had lost, he showed courage.

<u>To his children</u>, his courage might have come across as bravely ignoring what he couldn't do and instead focusing on what he could do—it taught them that life doesn't have to be easy to be lived well.

To his wife, his courage might have shown her that he would not let any obstacle get in the way of a successful marriage—it became a symbol of conquering adversity and the ability to build a satisfying life.

To his co-workers, his courage might have revealed that he had the perseverance to get through even the toughest of jobs—it showed that they could trust his inner strength.

To his community, his courage might have emerged in a city council fight for improving the safety of local streets despite very real financial and social obstacles—it gave others the audacity to continue this fight.

This idea-discovery process can be applied to almost anyone you want to honor through a eulogy. Certainly not everyone will have fully lived the virtue of courage, so, you can choose from a variety of other virtues and noble actions that represent the best of your loved one's life.

Selflessness: A woman who was both a divorced mother and a college student worked two jobs and took a leave of absence from her college studies so she could support her children when her former husband became unemployed and couldn't pay alimony or child support. She did these things without complaining or demeaning her children's father despite a difficult divorce.

Integrity: An uncle who worked as a journalist was jailed for several weeks because he wouldn't reveal one of his sources to the court. He believed that revealing his sources was contrary to his responsibilities as a journalist. In the end, his information wasn't necessary and he was released with a fine. Instead of complaining about the justice system, he simply said that he was proud to pay this price for doing his job with integrity.

Patience: A toddler suffered from cancer and a series of painful infections for most of her young life. She didn't often complain. Instead, she tried to make her parents laugh by making goofy faces. And she told them that even if she died, she knew she would be alright. (Chapter 6 talks more about eulogizing children.)

Obviously, the eulogy can use additional virtues and noble actions to say more good words about your loved one, illustrating his or her life even more fully. However, as the segment of Herb's original eulogy in this chapter shows, moderation is important. The eulogy needs to be both of a reasonable length and believable. If the eulogy is too long, mourners will tune it out. If someone is praised with too many strong adjectives and no examples to support the praise, listeners won't recognize the real person being eulogized, and the eulogy won't provide healing support for the bereaved.

In Herb's eulogy, for example, we see four virtues in one sentence: *"He headed a very large staff—all medical experts—yet, somehow he always managed to show humility, compassion, fairness, and decency."* What did that humility look like? Was he *always* compassionate? And always fair and decent? As the example revision shows, a more helpful approach would have been to choose one of these virtues and illustrate it by some biographical anecdotes. In this case, the virtue is humility. Although this drafted section wasn't actually included in the final revised eulogy, it demonstrates how to use biographical stories to demonstrate a single virtue in a believable way.

Showing Rather Than Telling: A Possible Revision for Herb's Eulogy

Herb was a good man, which we all could see in his humility. When someone introduced him by his professional title of "doctor," he simply asked that people call him by his first name. It's not that he wasn't proud of his professional degree, but more that he wanted to make others comfortable by knowing that they were talking to him—a man—and not his title. He was humble in other ways, too. In science writing, it's common to co-author articles with the first listed author being seen as the biggest contributor. But even when he was first author, Herb called attention to everyone else's singular and joint contributions. He made his colleagues feel valued.

This is a good time to examine a few of the deceased person's character qualities.

Using the space provided in appendix C's "Eulogy Writing Guide," write some of the virtues that you think most exemplify this person.

Ask yourself why or how you saw these qualities in his or her life and write down some of these ideas. Do the same thing for noble activities. Knowing that you probably won't use all of these character qualities in the actual eulogy, place checks by the ones that you think are most important to talk about. You might get family member's input here, too, as they'll likely have opinions about which character qualities best represent their loved one.

The following textboxes provide examples of how these notes might look. Ruth, my maternal aunt, died more than twenty years ago from cancer; although there was a memorial service in her church, there hasn't been a eulogy that the family could share. To learn more about Ruth, I talked with her three sisters. Therefore, the factual details, biographical stories, and character qualities or virtues that are recorded come primarily from their perspectives and memories, as well as my own perceptions of my aunt. Had I also talked with her children, these notes and the eulogy that developed from them (see appendix A) would have been somewhat different in content because the eulogy is shaped by loved ones' specific memories.

While talking with Ruth's sisters, I asked a few guiding questions in an attempt to learn as much as I could about my aunt. As they spoke, I jotted notes. Their responses naturally generated new questions and responses. I didn't worry about any particular order of questions or notes at that time. Some of the questions I asked were:

- When was Ruth born and when did she die? How did she die?
- What are your favorite memories of Ruth?
- Tell me a story about Ruth and someone in the family.
- As a child, what did your relationship with Ruth look like? What did you like about Ruth?
- Did Ruth have any special gifts (talents) or qualities (virtues) that she demonstrated throughout her lifetime?

My notes are recorded in the following three examples. They're in no particular order—just recorded as Ruth's sisters told them to me. How to organize the notes is covered in chapter 4.

Factual Details

- Ruth B.: deceased at 60 years old (Oct. 9, 1930 – Jan. 19, 1990)
- 1951 graduated from registered nursing training at Chester Hospital School of Nursing
- 40+ years of married life
- Colleen: 1 son, practical nurse
- Danny: 2 daughters and 1 son, carpenter
- Kevin: no children, iron work construction of bridges
- Graduated from Lancaster School of the Bible
- 3rd child of eight
- Died on a Thursday
- Uterine cancer, then breast cancer, then liver cancer
- Ashes in urn buried by favorite rock
- Ashes later placed in cemetery; Millard's later placed there although married a second time

Biographical Stories

- Majorette in high school; danced; very popular; voted cutest in class
- Violet and Donald bought her a graduation outfit that she still had when she died
- Face marred by glass after auto accident where neighbor was killed; car broke down; neighbor went to help; both hit by drunken driver;
- Ruth suffered at end of her life; slept in a reclining chair
- Fred visited and urged Violet to visit
- Early love in life was Homer, whom her father didn't like; they were like Mutt and Jeff
- Her Uncle Sam, who worked at Sun Oil during/after Depression, bought her and Violet new shoes; Ruth's shoes got wet and Violet decided to dry them in the oven; melted the rubber and Uncle Sam bought Ruth a new pair
- Violet failed first grade to go through school with Ruth, who was one year younger
- Had tuberculosis while carrying Danny
- Was sponsored at Faith Baptist Church; very Christian
- Yard sales: everyone friends but then every woman for herself
- Aluminum cans brought extra dollars
- Worked in Newport
- Creative, great seamstress, excellent knitter (argyle socks)
- Yellow Jacket and Greeley, Colorado; Blanchard, Idaho
- Hid extra money in books for rainy day
- Canned veggies and fruit; dried meat and salmon

Character Qualities

Virtues:

- Lived a good life; worked hard; happy woman
- She didn't carry a grudge (forgiving)
- She was fantastic in how she lived, loved, thought
- Tried to neuter a squirrel; it died; always curious
- Proverbs favorite book of Bible; knew Bible front to back

> **Noble activities**:
>
> - She always took care of the family of the neighbor who died while helping her; they never wanted for anything
> - At moment's notice, would grab doctor's bag and run to neighbors' to stitch up people and farm animals (cow's udder)
> - Taught Danny how to stitch up a person in case of hunting accident
> - Ruth planned to save $$ to send Daryl to nursing school, but marriage and children made saving impossible
> - Worked three jobs to help support husband Millard, who was poorly paid pastor

Step 3: Get Ready to Write the Eulogy

In this final step, begin to pull your notes together. You'll use what you've learned from family members and friends, as well as your own sense of the deceased. In addition, you can refer to example eulogies in appendix A.

Look back to the biographical stories and character qualities lists. First, read the checked notes to see whether you still want to talk about these things. Then, look at the notes without checks to see whether you've missed something important to connect the personal details, biographical stories, and character qualities that seem to go together. See what themes emerge from your notes.

For example, when I was writing about my father, I told a little bit of his early history as a child of immigrant parents to help connect his factual and biographical background (stories of accomplishment) with the virtues (integrity and commitment, expressed as purposefulness) that I wanted to highlight in the rest of the eulogy.

Connecting Factual and Biographical Background with Virtues: Example from My Father's Eulogy

We are here today to say goodbye to George J. C. L.

All of you have known him in some capacity—personal, professional, or community- related—and all of you had a place in his big heart.

To some of us he was family, to others a business associate, and to all he was a friend.

From modest beginnings, he shaped a life of great accomplishment. George, however, did not speak much about his beginnings and was similarly modest in professing his accomplishments. So, I will take a few moments to paint a portrait of a man whose life was full of accomplishments.

Born 65 short years ago in Brooklyn, New York, George was the son of Hungarian immigrants, Michael and Anna L. With his sister Elizabeth, the family worked hard and soon moved to Philadelphia, Pennsylvania. Finally, the family settled into suburban life in Folsom, Pennsylvania. Together, father and son built a fine brick home adjacent to his Uncle Charles' property.

George's life and character took shape in Folsom. He was full of boyish pranks—getting scolded by his parents and having mild skirmishes with this sister. He worked hard and played even harder—most notably, he was an excellent pinochle player. George's integrity and single-minded purposefulness were a part of his being at an early age.

In these lines, the facts of my father's life (age, cultural background, family names, and hometowns) combine with his stories (building a brick house with his father) to highlight the virtues that would take him through life. As the rest of his eulogy in appendix A shows, stories of his life were used to demonstrate his virtues and noble contributions to his family, co-workers, and community.

Using the appendix C "Eulogy Writing Guide," begin to write out connections among the factual details, biographical stories, and character qualities.

Chapter 4 explains how to organize these elements in the eulogy. Don't be afraid to work with the content that you've discovered in your talks with family and friends. Before you deliver the eulogy, you'll have a chance to share it with key people who can help you make any necessary corrections to facts, stories, and virtues.

Finding Good Words for Praising, Blessing, and Honoring

Praise in Difficult Relationships

There are situations when the praise of a traditional eulogy may not work. The grief that comes with the death of a loved one is hard enough to bear. Estrangements among family members and other difficult relationships can bring an even heavier sense of loss with the death of a loved one. Sometimes people just don't get along, and the resulting strained relationships can cause untold challenges for the bereaved.

> ❀ What good words can you say when you're conflicted about the person who has died?

> ❀ How can you say good things about this person if you haven't reached peace about whatever caused the problem?

Similarly difficult, some people simply haven't shown a great deal of virtue—or obvious virtue—in their lives.

> ❀ How can you write a eulogy about someone you generally didn't admire or didn't like or who didn't seem to demonstrate virtues and noble actions?

First, you don't need to be the person to write that eulogy. Get someone else to do it. When you're both grieving the loss and feeling upset with the deceased, it can be especially hard to find, let alone write, the best about that person.

Second, the traditional eulogy may not be the right venue for honoring the memory of certain individuals. Although I discuss this possibility below, let's look here at how even difficult relationships can lend themselves to traditional eulogies.

It's not a question of whether the deceased deserves a eulogy, but what will most help the bereaved recognize or pay tribute to the humanness of the deceased. It's helpful to remember that the person who has annoyed you in life is deeply loved and will be missed by others. It's a rare person who has been so unlikeable or evil that he or she won't have anyone mourning him or her. The truth is, the deceased wasn't perfect—as none of us are—but if there are loved ones left behind, they need to hear good words about their beloved family member or friend. After all, eulogies memorialize the dead, but they do so to the benefit of the living.

Even those deaths about which we're conflicted generally can lend themselves to discussing some virtue or noble action. There are times when the relationship among family members and the deceased is so strained that the family members don't recognize any virtues or noble actions. However, as they tell their stories, the eulogy writer may recognize some to highlight. For example, the deceased may have spent most weekends visiting his mother instead of his daughter and grandchildren. Understandably, the daughter may be upset, wishing for more of his attention and finding him to be lacking as a father and grandfather. Yet, a virtue that certainly emerges is that of dependability. This man could be depended upon by his mother to be there whenever she needed him. For her part, the chances are good that the daughter will recall at least one anecdote from a special time with her father, giving the writer both a virtue and a fond memory from his daughter.

Did you have a difficult relationship?

- Find another eulogy writer who can be more sympathetic to the deceased and his or her family.
- Look for at least one virtue and biographical story to help describe this person prior to bad years—maybe going back to childhood or adolescence.
- Consider a "blessing" rather than a traditional eulogy.

For another example, if a parent was abusive, alcoholic, mentally ill, or otherwise physically or emotionally unavailable, we usually can find a single act of courage or self-sacrifice that speaks well of the deceased. Perhaps a mother knew that her battle with schizophrenia was dangerous, so she tried to protect her daughter by teaching her the warning signs of an impending episode. Possibly an alcoholic father chose to leave home rather than inflict physical or emotional abuse on his children and wife; even though he chose to continue the harmful drinking behavior, he acted to try to protect them from inevitable hurt.

Praise in Difficult Situations

Conflict may arise at other times such as when the cause of death was one that society makes judgments about or finds embarrassing. When we're honest and open about the cause of death, particularly uncomfortable ones like suicide, AIDS, drug overdoses, alcoholism, or preventable accidents, we give the family public permission to talk about it without the unnecessary shame that often accompanies their grief. Honesty is important because the funeral and memorial ceremony is about acknowledging reality so that healing may begin. But if the family indicates that it is too hard to discuss such causes of death, it again may be best to move beyond the traditional eulogy to the blessing and honoring strategies that are discussed later in this chapter.

Suicide is a particularly difficult situation for a bereaved family and those who care about them. Although the relationship with the deceased may have been very good, a suicide rocks the foundations of that relationship, causing family members, friends, and co-workers to experience a range of emotions like guilt, anger, sadness, and frustration. They may not understand why the deceased took his or her life. These emotions should be acknowledged so that everyone—family included—knows that such feelings are common, normal, and nothing to be ashamed of. Because most funeral and memorial ceremonies come within a few days of the death, people may find themselves unready to deal with the suicide using straightforward language about it. They may not even realize as yet what they're actually feeling about this death. The following are a few words to acknowledge suicide, some of which are more indirect than others:

- Her sudden death
- He made a choice that we do not understand
- Her life has been lost to us
- When his life ended, ours changed forever
- She ended her life, and we don't know why

For example, if a teenager completed suicide, as eulogists we can acknowledge this cause of death without dwelling on it. Then, we can find praiseworthy virtues and noble deeds that help to define the adolescent's life from her position as a beloved child. The same kind of approach can be used when someone has overdosed on drugs or even unwittingly caused not only his or her own death but also the death of another person, as in an automobile accident.

My cousin Russ recently had the sad duty of delivering a eulogy for a friend and colleague who had died by suicide. He debated for several days whether he would deliver the eulogy and, if so, how. Up until the moment that he had to speak, he didn't know whether he could manage it. But he decided he must speak for the sake of his friend's wife and children, who needed to know how much their dad had loved them. Russ acknowledged Dave's sudden death and his own anger with Dave for not coming to him for help. He spoke of his own sense of guilt for not seeing his friend's depression. He addressed each child by name and told an anecdote that showed how much their father loved them. Russ talked about how no one would ever know why Dave had killed himself but that he and other mourners would remain available to talk with the family whenever they needed to. Then, he spoke about Dave's virtue of always helping others. He ended the eulogy with a spiritual story designed to help people transform their understanding of Dave's last hours:

Transformative Story Used to Bring Comfort to the Bereaved

Do you remember some years back, before 9/11, when you could go anywhere in the airport and watch people and planes come and go? If you wandered to the area where overseas travelers entered the United States, you would see people who were tired, scared, worn out already from trying to understand a language they didn't speak. They looked wearily at the masses of people greeting friends and family, and they felt too lost for words, but the droop of their shoulders and their worried faces showed their anxiety. Then, from the crowd, someone would call out their name or hold up a sign. And they knew at once where to go and with whom. They communicated, sometimes without words, and went to retrieve their bags.

Last Wednesday, my friend Dave came to a place where he'd never been before. He was tired. He was confused. He was in terrible pain. Despair was on his shoulders. A man came up to him and took him by the hand. All the bad things Dave was feeling went away— disappeared. And the man said: "Hi, Dave. My Father's house has many rooms. My name is Jesus, and I've come to take you home." Peace, David. We love you. Goodbye.

With that, Russ left the church and met the bereaved family again at the funeral reception.

On a connected note, many people who attempt or complete suicide do so while experiencing depression. Because depression is a clinically identifiable disease and because someone who suicides is in genuine pain, those who love a person who has died by suicide should seek professional help to better understand their loved one's condition and decision. Unfortunately, surviving another's suicide is a primary risk factor for attempting one's own suicide, particularly among at-risk groups like adolescents. Please seek out counseling and some of the excellent books and pamphlets available regarding grieving and understanding suicide.

When to Bless or Honor Rather Than Praise

As these examples suggest, any time that a virtue exists that can be praised, it seems best to write a traditional eulogy as described above. Although the eulogy may be short, the fact that good words are expressed can be tremendously healing. It's helpful to note that the length of the eulogy isn't as important as its content and goals of remembering the deceased and supporting the bereaved.

However, it's also true that deaths related to difficult relationships and situations can create ambivalent feelings in mourners, which can make them unreceptive to the praises of a traditional eulogy. Here, the difference between the ideas of *praising*, *blessing*, and *honoring* become important because even when we find it difficult to praise a life, we can bless or honor the deceased with good words and love. In other words, we can dislike what the person has done while still loving the person—or at least acknowledging his or her common human nature in a nonjudgmental way.

Basically, the act of praising signals a comparison. We include praise-worthy behavior and character traits in a eulogy, generally ignoring what isn't praise worthy because the funeral or memorial ceremony isn't the time or place to explore these issues. Time-wise, that necessary grief work should happen after the ceremony and not during it. Place-wise, grief support groups, individual therapy sessions, and intimate family settings can be appropriate for addressing those concerns.

Praise expressed in a eulogy is *about* the deceased; blessings and honoring are expressed *for* or *to* the deceased (and the bereaved). As opposed to praising, the act of blessing or honoring signals a non-judgmental sentiment.

The word "blessing" usually has a spiritual meaning, and we tend to think about a religious setting when we hear this word. In religious contexts, a blessing is conferred by a person who is officially vested with spiritual responsibilities, such as a minister, priest, pastor, rabbi, or monk. Not all religions confer blessings, seeing them as coming only from God or a Higher Power, so it's best to check with your religion's clergy on this point.

Often, a blessing suggests a belief in a spiritual afterlife whereby the deceased's soul or essence is sent forth to the next level of existence. However, *blessing* also means "to wish well." In this context, as I explained in chapter 1, everyday people like you and me can offer a blessing that wishes peace and spiritual well-being for both the deceased and those who are grieving.

If you don't believe in God or any Higher Power, however, the concept of blessing the deceased may not feel right to you. And if the deceased was known to be an atheist or agnostic, he or she might have objected to the word "blessing" being used in the ceremony. In these cases, use the word "honor" to think about how to offer good wishes.

Whichever word you use, the idea is similar: everyone can be memorialized because of our shared human nature. All humans have deep yearnings and needs, and we all search for something in our lifetime. All humans seek love and some degree of connection. In these commonalities, we can empathize with the bereaved by honoring the one who has died. Indeed, when a person's life has ended in way that is difficult to praise, blessing and honoring are especially important and validating to everyone who attends the gathering.

Beyond the official blessings conferred by clergy, virtually anyone can bless or honor the deceased as it can take various secular forms. These acts show respect for the human life that will be connected eternally to mourners and that, for whatever reason, was cut short before all of its potential had been reached.

How to Bless and Honor

There are a variety of ways that we can memorialize people who are difficult to praise in a traditional eulogy.

First, plan to make the eulogy short. Using steps 1 and 2 listed earlier in this chapter, consult with family members and gently seek information about the deceased. People are likely to recall something good about this person in childhood or adolescence before life's challenges brought him or her down. If there's a virtue that emerges, use it to develop a more traditional eulogy. If not, try telling a biographical story about him or her that shows the innocence or delight of a child. Remember that it's the family who most needs to hear these good words. Appendix B presents a eulogy that blesses and honors my sister after her unfortunate battle with addiction.

> **Bless or Honor the Deceased Especially If the Person:**
>
> - Died unrepentant in prison
> - Deliberately harmed another person
> - Acted in a way that family or society considers wrong
> - Has been estranged from family for a long time
> - Made foolish life choices that harmed himself or others

Second, using the distinctions outlined above, decide whether it seems best to bless or honor this person.

There are many examples of blessings available in books and on the Internet. For example, traditional funeral blessings that lay people often use include participatory readings, psalms, and spiritual poetry. In this example from the Jewish tradition, the reading asks the gathered mourners to join by reciting the italicized phrase "we remember them."

From the Gates of Prayer – Reform Judaism Prayer Book

At the rising sun and at its going down, *we remember them.*

At the blowing of the wind and in the chill of winter, *we remember them.*

At the opening of the buds and in the rebirth of spring, *we remember them.*

At the blueness of the skies and in the warmth of summer, *we remember them.*

At the rustling of the leaves and in the beauty of the autumn, *we remember them.*

At the beginning of the year and when it ends, *we remember them.*

As long as we live, they too will live;

For they are now a part of us, as *we remember them.*

When we are weary and in need of strength, *we remember them.*

When we are lost and sick at heart, *we remember them.*

When we have decisions that are difficult to make, *we remember them.*

When we have joy we crave to share, *we remember them.*

When we have achievements that are based on theirs, *we remember them.*

For as long as we live, they too will live;

For they are now a part of us, as *we remember them.*

There are many poems that can be read aloud to express some of your spiritual thoughts and sentiments for the deceased and/or the bereaved. Some examples include "To All Parents" and "As We Prayed" by Edgar Guest. Appendix B provides additional complete examples of readings and poetry for blessing a loved one.

To honor the deceased and for the bereaved who wish to use more secular sentiments, you might read the poem provided below or any of those listed under "honoring" in appendix B. Similar poems include "The Ship of Life" by John T. Baker, "Funeral Blues" by W. H. Auden, and "Missed," and "Sharing" by Edgar Guest, most of which can be found in an Internet or library search. Or, you could ask the family whether there is a special book that she loved to read or a hobby that he especially enjoyed. If so, choose a reading from that book or a brief segment about the noble or fun nature of the hobby. These kinds of readings are secular in nature and don't imply any particular spiritual belief system.

Remember
by Christina Georgina Rossetti

Remember me when I am gone away,
Gone far away into the silent land;
When you can no more hold me by the hand,
Nor I half turn to go, yet turning stay.
Remember me when no more, day by day,
You tell me of our future that you planned:
Only remember me; you understand
It will be late to counsel then or pray.
Yet if you should forget me for a while
And afterwards remember, do not grieve:
For if the darkness and corruption leave
A vestige of the thoughts that I once had,
Better by far you should forget and smile
Than that you should remember and be sad.

Other ideas for blessings and honors include:

- Leading an opportunity for everyone to state a good wish for the deceased while lighting a candle or taking/giving a rose or other flower
- Giving the mourners a memento of the deceased like a prayer card, handmade butterfly, or copy of a poem
- Playing a special piece of music and providing the lyrics to the gathered people
- Singing a well-known song together

Chapter 4

How Do I Organize These Good Words?

Once you've decided what details to share about the deceased, you need to figure out where in the eulogy you'll say these things. This chapter will help you to decide where to use the ideas that you discovered in your notes taken in chapter 3. The focus is on organizing the content in effective ways. Figuring out "where" to say the good words is the task of arrangement.

Like any other speech, the typical eulogy has at least three parts: (1) an introduction that suggests a theme; (2) a body section of a narrative story or stories, illustrative details, and examples; and (3) a conclusion to draw everything together.

Introductions

Writers sometimes have anxiety about the opening of the eulogy because they want to grab and keep fellow mourners' attention for a few minutes during a time when they might be very distracted. People attending the funeral may be talking with others or wandering in their own thoughts of the deceased. Sometimes it's hard to know where to start. In fact, sometimes people write the introduction last—after they've seen where the eulogy has gone in terms of ideas.

What does the introduction generally do? It might:

- Give specifics about the deceased like the name, age and/or marital and parenting status
- Say something about the occasion and purpose for the eulogy (for example, that everyone is engaged in a ceremony to honor the deceased)
- Highlight the deceased's main virtues (that is, the ones you'll be talking about)
- Indicate how the eulogy is organized (that is, what to expect next)
- Address your relationship to the deceased.

To begin to do these things, a eulogy often uses what is called a "ritual" or "ceremonial" opening. For example, when most Americans hear the words "we are gathered here today to celebrate…," the next words they think of likely will be "the union of this man and this woman." The exact wording might differ, of course, but the idea of a wedding or marriage ceremony usually is conveyed by these ritual words. Sometimes, people both grieve their loss *and* celebrate the life of the deceased, and that intention can be communicated with those same words: "we are gathered here to celebrate the life of Jane Doe." Similarly, when people hear the words "we are gathered here to mourn…," the next words likely will be "the passing of John Doe" or "the death of our dear friend Mary Doe" or something similar. Ritual openings are helpful because they center the audience in what is happening at that point of the ceremony—they know that a sermon, homily, or eulogy is going to follow, and they get ready to listen.

Another way to begin a eulogy—oddly enough—is with self-reference. Speakers who deliver a eulogy may not be comfortable with public speaking, but they may be the best person for that job for a variety of reasons. At such times, speakers may be nervous or feel unworthy to be presenting the eulogy. Would it surprise you to know that people have felt that way about delivering eulogies for thousands of years? The ancient rhetoricians of Greece and Rome, who were paid public speakers, often opened a eulogy with words indicating that they didn't see themselves as the best person for the job. In today's lingo, they might say:

- "Although I didn't know Jane as well as Tom and Selma did, I've been asked to speak to you about her life."

- "Even though I am a minister, I realized that my own words are inadequate for talking about the ways that John's life has influenced others. So, I turned to my grandmother's wisdom and the advice she once gave me about the rare specialness of some people. Her advice seems fitting for us who mourn John."

- "Who can know best how to appropriately honor a person who was as strong and brave as Mary? Certainly not me, but I will try to do that anyway."

There are other proven introduction patterns that can help you to decide how to begin the eulogy. These patterns include:

- Citing a quotation, poem, or song lyrics
- Relating an anecdote or story
- Beginning with a question
- Making a simple statement of fact

Here are some example introductions from eulogies honoring historically famous individuals. Notice how each eulogy begins with some kind of ritual opening and a statement about the inadequacy of words when speaking about the deceased:

Eulogy Introductions

We come together today to mourn the loss of seven brave Americans, to share the grief we all feel and, perhaps in that sharing, to find the strength to bear our sorrow and the courage to look for the seeds of hope.

Our nation's loss is first a profound personal loss to the family and the friends and loved ones of our Shuttle astronauts. To those they have left behind—the mothers, the fathers, the husbands and wives, brothers, sisters, and yes, especially the children—all of America stands beside you in your time of sorrow.

What we say today is only an inadequate expression of what we carry in our hearts. Words pale in the shadow of grief; they seem insufficient even to measure the brave sacrifice of those you loved and we so admired. Their truest testimony will not be in the words we speak, but in the way they led their lives and in the way they lost those lives—with dedication, honor and an unquenchable desire to explore this mysterious and beautiful universe. (Spoken by then-President Ronald Reagan on the occasion of eulogizing the astronauts of the space shuttle Challenger.)

Mr. President, <u>hundreds of thousands of words have been published, and hundreds of thousands more have been spoken into the microphones of the world</u> since John F. Kennedy was struck down in Dallas, <u>but none of them were really adequate.</u> Words never are in the face of senseless tragedy. (Spoken by Senator Jacob Javits on the occasion of eulogizing President John F. Kennedy.)

<u>I stand before you today the representative of a family in grief, in a country in mourning before a world in shock.</u> We are all united not only in our desire to pay our respects to Diana but rather in our need to do so. For such was her extraordinary appeal that the tens of millions of people taking part in this service all over the world via television and radio who never actually met her, feel that they too lost someone close to them in the early hours of Sunday morning. It is a more remarkable tribute to Diana than I can ever hope to offer her today. (Spoken by Earl Charles Spencer on the occasion of eulogizing Princess Diana.)

The eulogy that you will write can begin in similar ways. You don't need to develop a brand new or especially creative opening to get people's attention. They expect and readily accept a ritual opening.

<u>We're gathered here today to mourn the death and celebrate the life of George L.,</u> beloved husband, father, son, brother, and friend. A week ago, had you asked any of us what we would be doing on this summer afternoon, none of us would have guessed that we would be attending George's funeral. (Spoken by a close friend on the occasion of eulogizing George J. L.)

Feel free to use these openings and those of the eulogies presented in appendix A as models and prompts for introducing the eulogy you're writing.

The Body of the Eulogy

The body of the eulogy is a narration of the deceased's life. It's the most crucial part of the speech. This is where you use the biographical stories you gathered earlier. As chapter 3 discusses, the narrative tells about the deceased's life and influence on others—the virtues and noble actions that most represent this person. It illustrates a person's life through examples, stories, and testimonies from those who knew the deceased. Not surprisingly, there are various ways to arrange the body of the eulogy. The choice you make depends on the story you want to tell.

Organizational strategies include arranging by:

- Chronology, or timeframes within a person's life, that demonstrate how one has grown or developed:
    - Earliest to most recent years
    - Recent to earliest years (reverse chronology)
- Events that the deceased experienced or that he or she caused, as well as the effects of these events:
    - Critical events that shaped the person
    - Deeds that the person performed
- Influence on others, including the world at large:
    - A person's influence on family and friends
    - How people will remember the deceased
- Themes that represent important virtues:
    - How the deceased learned these virtues
    - How the virtues were demonstrated in the deceased's life

Each of these organizational strategies is demonstrated on the following pages through different arrangements of my notes for my Aunt Ruth (see chapter 3). Recall that as her sisters spoke to me, I jotted notes and didn't worry about any particular order. In this next step of my writing process, I reviewed my notes and underlined words that indicated virtues because they are primary characteristics on which the eulogy should focus (see the textbox called "Notes for Ruth").

The pages following "Notes for Ruth" show how I outlined the notes using different organizational approaches. I dropped or added some details from one outline to the next when it seemed like they wouldn't fit the emerging story. The outlines below illustrate each of the arrangement strategies that are discussed above.

The first set of notes is organized in terms of *chronology* from youth to later years.

Notes for Ruth (with virtues underlined)

- Ruth: deceased at 60 years old (Oct. 9, 1930 – Jan. 19, 1990)
- Majorette in high school; danced; very popular; voted cutest in class
- 1951 graduated from registered nursing training at Chester Hospital School of Nursing
- Violet and Donald bought her a graduation outfit that she still had when she died
- Lived a good life; worked hard; happy woman
- Face marred by glass after auto accident where neighbor was killed; car broke down; neighbor went to help; both hit by drunken driver; she always took care of his family
- Ruth suffered at end of her life; slept in a reclining chair
- Fred visited and urged Violet to visit
- Died on a Thursday
- Early love in life was Homer, whom her father didn't like; they were like Mutt and Jeff
- 40+ years of married life
- She didn't carry a grudge (forgiving)
- Her Uncle Sam, who worked at Sun Oil during/after Depression, bought her and Violet new shoes; Ruth's shoes got wet and Violet decided to dry them in the oven; melted the rubber and Uncle Sam bought Ruth a new pair
- 3rd child of eight
- Violet failed first grade to go through school with Ruth, who was one year younger

---

- Colleen: 1 son, practical nurse
- Danny: 2 daughters and 1 son, carpenter
- Kevin: no children, iron work construction of bridges
- She was fantastic in how she lived, loved, thought
- At moment's notice, would grab doctor's bag and run to neighbors' to stitch up people and farm animals (cow's udder)
- Had tuberculosis while carrying Danny
- Tried to neuter a squirrel; it died; always curious
- Taught Danny how to stitch up a person in case of hunting accident
- Ashes in urn buried by favorite rock
- Ruth planned to save $$ to send Daryl to nursing school, but marriage and children made saving impossible
- Was sponsored at Faith Baptist Church; very Christian
- Yard sales: everyone friends but then every woman for herself
- Aluminum cans brought extra dollars
- Graduated from Lancaster School of the Bible Uterine cancer, then breast cancer, then liver cancer
- Worked in Newport
- Creative, great seamstress, excellent knitter (argyle socks)
- Proverbs favorite book of Bible; knew Bible front to back
- Yellow Jacket and Greeley, Colorado; Blanchard, Idaho
- Hid extra money in books for rainy day
- Canned veggies and fruit; dried meat and salmon
- Worked three jobs to help support husband Millard, who was poorly paid pastor
- Ashes later placed in cemetery; Millard's later placed there although married a second time

The second set of notes is arranged in terms of *primary events* in Ruth's life.

Events Influencing Ruth's Life

- Ruth: deceased at 60 years old (Oct. 9, 1930 – Jan. 19, 1990)
- She was fantastic in how she lived, loved, thought
- Lived a good life; worked hard; happy woman

Childhood
- 3rd child of eight
- Early love in life was Homer, whom her father didn't like; they were like Mutt and Jeff
- Majorette in high school; danced; very popular; voted cutest in class

Faith
- Was sponsored at Faith Baptist Church; very Christian
- Graduated from Lancaster School of the Bible
- Proverbs favorite book of Bible; knew Bible front to back

Accident
- Face marred by glass after auto accident where neighbor was killed; car broke down; neighbor went to help; both hit by drunken driver; she always took care of his family
- She didn't carry a grudge

Family
- Colleen: 1 son, practical nurse
- Danny: 2 daughters and 1 son, carpenter
- Had tuberculosis while carrying Danny
- Kevin: no children, iron work construction of bridges
- At moment's notice, would grab doctor's bag and run to neighbors' to stitch up people and farm animals (cow's udder)
- Tried to neuter a squirrel; it died; always curious
- Taught Danny how to stitch up a person in case of hunting accident
- Yellow Jacket and Greeley, Colorado; Blanchard, Idaho

Work for family
- 1951 graduated from registered nursing training at Chester Hospital School of Nursing

---

- Worked three jobs to help support husband Millard, who was poorly paid pastor
- Yard sales: everyone friends but then every woman for herself
- Aluminum cans brought extra dollars
- Worked in Newport
- Creative, great seamstress, excellent knitter (argyle socks)
- Hid extra money in books for rainy day
- Canned veggies and fruit; dried meat and salmon

Illness and death

- Uterine cancer, then breast cancer, then liver cancer
- Ruth suffered at end of her life; slept in a reclining chair
- Fred visited and urged Violet to visit
- Died on a Thursday
- 40+ years of married life
- Ashes in urn buried by favorite rock
- Ashes later placed in cemetery; Millard's later placed there although married a second time

The third set of notes is arranged in terms of Ruth's *influence on others*.

Ruth's Influence On Others

- Ruth: deceased at 60 years old (Oct. 9, 1930 – Jan. 19, 1990)
- She was fantastic in how she lived, loved, thought
- Lived a good life; worked hard; happy woman
- Proverbs favorite book of Bible; knew Bible front to back

Immediate family

- 1951 graduated from registered nursing training at Chester Hospital School of Nursing
- Colleen: 1 son, practical nurse
- Danny: 2 daughters and 1 son, carpenter
- Had tuberculosis while carrying Danny
- Kevin: no children, iron work construction of bridges
- Tried to neuter a squirrel; it died; always curious
- Taught Danny how to stitch up a person in case of hunting accident
- Creative, great seamstress, excellent knitter (argyle socks)
- Hid extra money in books for rainy day
- Canned veggies and fruit; dried meat and salmon
- Worked three jobs to help support husband Millard, who was poorly paid pastor
- Yard sales: everyone friends but then every woman for herself
- Aluminum cans brought extra dollars

Extended family

- Her Uncle Sam, who worked at Sun Oil during/after Depression, bought her and Violet new shoes; Ruth's shoes got wet and Violet decided to dry them in the oven; melted the rubber and Uncle Sam bought Ruth a new pair
- 3rd child of eight
- Violet failed first grade to go through school with Ruth, who was one year younger
- Was sponsored at Faith Baptist Church; very Christian
- Early love in life was Homer, whom her father didn't like; they were like Mutt and Jeff
- Majorette in high school; danced; very popular; voted cutest in class

---

- Violet and husband Donald bought her a graduation outfit that she still had when she died
- Ruth planned to save $$ to send sister Daryl to nursing school, but marriage and children made saving impossible

Community at large
- Graduated from Lancaster School of the Bible
- Yellow Jacket and Greeley, Colorado; Blanchard, Idaho
- At moment's notice, would grab doctor's bag and run to neighbors' to stitch up people and farm animals (cow's udder)
- Worked in Newport
- Face marred by glass after auto accident where neighbor was killed; car broke down; neighbor went to help; both hit by drunken driver; she always took care of his family
- She didn't carry a grudge

Conclusion
- Uterine cancer, then breast cancer, then liver cancer
- Ruth suffered at end of her life; slept in a reclining chair
- Fred visited and urged Violet to visit
- Died on a Thursday
- 40+ years of married life
- Ashes in urn buried by favorite rock
- Ashes later placed in cemetery; Millard's later placed there although married a second time

Finally, the fourth set of notes is organized in terms of *themes* that demonstrate Ruth's virtues. This is the organization that I chose for the final eulogy (see appendix A).

Virtues and Themes in Ruth's Life
Used "Book of Wisdom/Proverbs" for Organization

- Ruth: deceased at 60 years old (Oct. 9, 1930 – Jan. 19, 1990)
- She was fantastic in how she lived, loved, thought
- Lived a good life; worked hard; happy woman
- Proverbs favorite book of Bible; knew Bible front to back

The praises of others
- 3rd child of eight
- Early love in life was Homer, whom her father didn't like; they were like Mutt and Jeff
- Majorette in high school; danced; very popular; voted cutest in class

A lamp from the Lord
- 1951 graduated from registered nursing training at Chester Hospital School of Nursing
- Graduated from Lancaster School of the Bible
- Yellow Jacket and Greeley, Colorado; Blanchard, Idaho
- Had tuberculosis while carrying Danny

A worthy wife
- At moment's notice, would grab doctor's bag and run to neighbors' to stitch up people and farm animals (cow's udder)

Homemaking
- Worked three jobs to help support husband Millard, who was poorly paid pastor
- Worked in Newport
- Aluminum cans brought extra dollars
- Creative, great seamstress, excellent knitter (argyle socks)
- Hid extra money in books for rainy day
- Canned veggies and fruit; dried meat and salmon
- Colleen: 1 son, practical nurse
- Danny: 2 daughters and 1 son, carpenter
- Kevin: no children, iron work construction of bridges

Reaching out to others

- Yard sales: everyone friends but then every woman for herself
- Face marred by glass after auto accident where neighbor was killed; car broke down; neighbor went to help; both hit by drunken driver; she always took care of his family
- She didn't carry a grudge

Strength and dignity

- Uterine cancer, then breast cancer, then liver cancer
- Ruth suffered at end of her life; slept in a reclining chair
- Fred visited and urged Violet to visit
- Died on a Thursday

Praise and love of children and husband

- 40+ years of married life
- Ashes in urn buried by favorite rock
- Ashes later placed in cemetery; Millard's later placed there although married a second time

When deciding how to organize the body of the eulogy, it may help you to look at your information from different perspectives as the different outlines of these notes show. The approach you choose will depend on the type of information you have about the deceased, your relationship to that person, and what you want others to know about him or her.

Conclusions

Once the body of the eulogy has been drafted, it needs a conclusion. The conclusion provides a sense of closure and emotional satisfaction about the deceased's life. The eulogy's conclusion symbolizes that a life has ended, just as it signals to the gathered mourners that the next part of the ceremony will begin.

Sometimes, once you get started writing, the eulogy will take on a life of its own. It will simply *write itself,* and the conclusion will emerge from your mind as the perfect ending. If that happens, enjoy the beautiful way that words sometimes come together. However, if you need help with the conclusion, it's useful to know that there are ritual ways of ending a eulogy.

Just like there are established organizational patterns for the content of the introduction and the body, there also are conclusion patterns. These include:

- Explaining why the mourners should think favorably about the deceased
- Asking questions, making comparisons, or otherwise reminding the audience of the loved one's chief praise-worthy characteristics
- Encouraging people to emulate these attributes, which is a way of minimizing more negative traits
- Calling on a common conception of God or a Higher Power for consolation and blessing
- Using emotional cues that move the audience to react with sorrow, pity, indignation, and even laughter

The following are some example endings to eulogies of famous people. They demonstrate a few of these ways to draw the eulogy to a close.

Eulogy Conclusion 1

In a real sense we, his former colleagues in the Congress, are the only ones with the power to write words which can transform these aspirations into memorials with meaning. We can write legislative acts, like a meaningful civil rights law, which would consecrate and perpetuate John F. Kennedy's love for personal and national dignity. We can exorcise from our country—and the American people are doing that even now—those extremes of hatred and disbelief in public affairs which create a climate in which terrible acts become much more likely.

Acts such as these will be his final memorials. It is within our power to establish them. Perhaps his noblest memorial is that he would have wanted such memorials almost as no others.

So, in common with my colleagues in this solemn service—and that is what this is today—I bespeak for Mrs. Javits and my children—and I would place their names in the Record, so that as they read this Record when they grow up, I hope they will read their names in it and see that their father spoke with deep sympathy--Joy, Joshua, and Carla, to Mrs. Kennedy and the children, and to the president's father and mother and his brothers and sisters and their families our deepest sympathy on this terrible bereavement, for our nation and for all mankind, and in the deep expectation that flowers will grow from his grave for the benefit of man. (Spoken by Senator Jacob Javits on the occasion of eulogizing President John F. Kennedy.)

In this example from John F. Kennedy's eulogy, notice how Javits urges his colleagues in Congress to enact the kinds of legislation that would make the deceased president proud of his country. This is the congressman's way of calling on his listeners to emulate Kennedy as the most meaningful tribute to his life and death.

In this next example, Earl Charles Spencer, brother of Princess Diana, uses a ritual ending (that is, "I would like to end..."), calls on God in thanksgiving, and names what he believes are positive things about Princess Diana's death. In doing so, he takes the incredible sadness of the day and suggests that the listeners will one day find peace around their common bereavement. Spencer then reiterates Princess Diana's virtues for which she will be long remembered.

Eulogy Conclusion 2

I would like to end by thanking God for the small mercies he has shown us at this dreadful time. For taking Diana at her most beautiful and radiant and when she had joy in her private life. Above all we give thanks for the life of a woman I am so proud to be able to call my sister, the unique, the complex, the extraordinary and irreplaceable Diana whose beauty, both internal and external, will never be extinguished from our minds. (Spoken by Earl Charles Spencer on the occasion of eulogizing Princess Diana.)

President Reagan speaks for the American people in this next example. The ending of his eulogy for the Challenger astronauts includes a promise of continuing support for NASA's space program. More than that, he likens the lost astronauts to heroes who will be commemorated by America's future space quests (much like Javits urged Congress to enact great legislation). The call to continue to do something with our remaining lifetime is a common and effective way of concluding a eulogy because it reaffirms that we need to continue living in positive ways. Reagan ends by invoking God, much as Spencer does, because belief in or desire to know God is often strongest in the face of a tragedy.

Eulogy Conclusion 3

Today, we promise Dick Scobee and his crew that their dream lives on; that the future they worked so hard to build will become reality. The dedicated men and women of NASA have lost seven members of their family. Still, <u>they too, must forge ahead</u>, with a space program that is effective, safe and efficient, but bold and committed.

<u>Man will continue his conquest of space.</u> To reach out for new goals and ever greater achievements—that is the way we shall commemorate our seven Challenger heroes.

Dick, Mike, Judy, El, Ron, Greg and Christa—your families and your country mourn your passing. We bid you goodbye. We will never forget you. For those who knew you well and loved you, the pain will be deep and enduring. A nation, too, will long feel the loss of her seven sons and daughters, her seven good friends. We can find consolation only in faith, <u>for we know in our hearts that you who flew so high and so proud now</u> <u>make your home beyond the stars, safe in God's promise of eternal life.</u>

May God bless you all and give you comfort in this difficult time. (Spoken by President Ronald Reagan on the occasion of eulogizing the Challenger astronauts.)

Finally, a eulogy can evoke laughter with tasteful humor, as in my brother's eulogy and the tales of his misadventures. However, even humor can create a space for more tears. As chapter 2 explains, tears are important emotional expressions of grief, and it is no shame to cry during (and after) funeral and memorial ceremonies. Whenever I read the final paragraph of my brother's George's eulogy (shown below), my throat has a catch in it and I tear up. That's not because I wrote it but because the poem about flying that is cited connects perfectly to the God that George so loved.[3]

Evoking Emotions in the Conclusion

And so, as we mourn George and celebrate his life, let us not be angry with him for his love of speed and his love of flying, for those loves combined to make him who he was. Let us say, along with him, "Oh, I

---

[3] Taken from "High Flight" by John Gillespie Magee, Jr.; coincidentally, Ronald Reagan also cited this poem in the eulogy for the Challenger astronauts.

have slipped the surly bonds of earth, And danced the skies on laughter silvered wings." George, when you touch the face of God, please say hello to Him for us. (Spoken by a close friend on the occasion of eulogizing George J. L.)

Poems, songs, and any kind of artwork or object of beauty can be joined helpfully to the deceased's ideas about the afterlife to suggest the potential for his or her happiness outside of this life.

This chapter has explained and illustrated how to organize the eulogy. Introduction and conclusion choices not only have ritual words that you can use, but they're also developed to evoke some kind of feeling or reaction from the audience. The body of the eulogy is used to tell the story of the deceased's life in whatever organization seems most suited to the information you've gathered.

Chapter 7 further explains how to develop an eloquent eulogy by illustrating some things about style—how to say things gracefully and memorably. If you're pressed for time, skip this chapter for now. However, quite often the bereaved family members and friends appreciate a print copy of the eulogy for sharing and tucking away with mementos of their loved one. In that case, take some time when you're not in a hurry to use chapter 7's information for polishing the eulogy.

Chapter 5

How Do I Deliver These Good Words?

Delivery means to read or speak the eulogy aloud. Most often, people read the eulogy as it was written, although some people are more comfortable speaking from talking points or notes. This chapter offers practical guidance for delivering the eulogy eloquently and powerfully. Elements of delivery include how to prepare, what and where to practice, elements of delivery style for maximum effect, and speaking from notes.

Choosing the Right Person to Deliver the Eulogy

Preparing to deliver a eulogy begins before the actual funeral or memorial ceremony, and sometimes it even begins before writing a single word. Preparation actually begins with the vital act of choosing a speaker.

Quite often, the eulogy writer is also the speaker. In that case, it's likely that the eulogy itself will match the writer/speaker's own personal character and style. In this case, the writer has himself or herself in mind as a speaker and knows how the eulogy should sound.

On the other hand, sometimes a eulogist will write the eulogy for someone else to deliver. When the designated speaker and the eulogist are not the same person, the writer needs to talk with the speaker as early as possible about the content of the eulogy and how the writer thinks it might be delivered. It's equally important to know something about the speaker's personality in order to match the eulogy's style to the speaker's style.

Who might be the "right" person to read the eulogy? Knowing something about the speaker's personal qualities and character may help when selecting someone to deliver the eulogy.

- Did this person know the deceased very well?

- Is this person an especially effective or comfortable speaker in other settings or situations?

- Is this person poised, confident, dignified, and likely to be able to contain his or her strongest emotions?

Choosing the Right Speaker to Deliver the Eulogy

This second scenario was the case for both my brother's and father's eulogies. Although I was able to read a poem at my father's service with some degree of self-control, I knew I couldn't read the eulogy without becoming highly emotional. If I or a sibling had tried, the audience wouldn't have been thinking about our brother or father, but about us.

While not everyone feels this way, given our shock at their sudden deaths, we believed that our primary role at these services was simply to be who we were—bereaved family members. So, in these cases, we asked family friends—a different one for each funeral—to be speakers. We chose my brother's best friend because he knew and loved my brother so well. But we chose my cousin to speak for our father because Russ is a refined and believable speaker.

- Has this person volunteered to help out by organizing ceremony details or otherwise carrying messages for the family?

In the ancient world, Cicero called the "orator" or "speaker" a "good man speaking well." By that, he meant that a speaker should be a person of good character—someone who the audience might know as an admirable person with virtuous qualities of his or her own. The speaker's qualities are important because the audience will listen more closely to someone that they know to have integrity. Some of these qualities might include:

- Believability as someone who knew and respected the deceased
- Being someone who has had a close relationship with the deceased and the surviving family
- Personal qualities of virtue and noble actions

Even when only a few people in the audience know the speaker, the fact that the bereaved family has chosen him or her to deliver the eulogy conveys that they trust this person with a tribute to their beloved family member.

Other variables include the speaker's age, maturity, and experience in speaking publicly. First, when working with an elderly speaker, check in with him or her regarding the physical and emotional pressure of public speaking during the stress of the funeral or memorial ceremony. Indeed, anyone who may seem overwhelmed might find delivering a eulogy to be especially trying; it would be wise to have a back-up speaker in this case. However, whether the person has the potential to "break down" isn't the best reason for selecting or rejecting a speaker because any speaker could cry during a eulogy. Emotions are a natural response to the sadness of most funeral and memorial ceremonies. Although crying is perfectly understandable, some people grieve more expressively. It's wise to avoid the potential for such demonstrative grief as it will take attention away from the eulogy.

Second, consider maturity when choosing a speaker. Asking (or allowing) children and teenagers to speak the eulogy may subject them to pressures beyond what they are able to manage. Because death affects children differently from adults, children and eulogies are the subjects of chapter 6. Maturity also reveals itself in the speaker's choice of clothing, which should be respectful and appropriately somber. Although black isn't required at most American contemporary services, dark or muted colors for suits and dresses still are considered appropriate, as is clothing that is less revealing than you might see at a teen dance.

Third, on a very practical level, consider whether the speaker expresses a reasonable comfort level with public speaking and/or reading aloud, as well as his or her vocal range and interpretative abilities. It's best to recruit a speaker who reads well and is able to both read and modulate the voice at the same time. Because the eulogy has the potential to help the bereaved to begin their mourning formally, it can lead them to a healing path. If it is spoken poorly or with insufficient dignity, however, the eulogy can leave people feeling somewhat numb and, at worst, it can cause them anger or frustration that their beloved deceased hasn't been sufficiently honored. The choice of the right speaker can be a powerful one that allows the good words of the eulogy to convey the intended message.

What and Where to Practice

At this point, the eulogy has been written and the speaker has been chosen. Ideally, the written eulogy will be completed at least several hours before the ceremony, if not sooner. When the eulogy is to be delivered by someone other than the writer, email is an excellent way to get it to the speaker ahead of time. The speaker needs a chance to practice the eulogy aloud and away from the funeral setting, if possible. He or she also needs the chance to read it silently several times to learn the nuances of the speech as it is written. Reading it both aloud and silently allows the speaker to figure out what works stylistically. It may be necessary to vary some sentences or phrases to make the eulogy sound natural to him or her. If it doesn't sound natural to the speaker, then some of the writer's care and thoughtfulness might be lost in the delivery. While it isn't necessary to memorize a eulogy, it's helpful for the speaker to be completely familiar with it before the ceremony.

Here are several helpful steps for practicing the eulogy:

Make the eulogy easy to read.

- Print out a typed copy of the eulogy.
- Use a large font of about 16-18 points.
- Use an easy-to-read font like Arial or Calibri to help guide the reader's eye from letter to letter and from word to word.
- Double space between each line and triple space between each paragraph.

After practicing by yourself, read the eulogy aloud to another person.

🙚 Ask this person for feedback on clarity of speech—whether you can be understood—and voice tone.

🙚 This practice, if done shortly before the ceremony, should be in a room other than where the bereaved family and guests are gathering.

🙚 Be familiar enough with the eulogy to look up from the page occasionally and make eye contact with someone in the audience.

Know where you are going to speak.

🙚 Is there a podium? It's a good idea to be standing in a slightly elevated place like on a platform or at a podium. This elevation will make it easier for the seated audience to see you and your voice will project much better from a raised standing position.

🙚 Can you have a microphone? Whenever possible, use a microphone to help you modulate your voice. Voices can be difficult to hear when strong emotions arise.

At the podium:

🙚 Have an extra copy of the eulogy placed there for you. Ask to have water there or nearby.

🙚 Put some tissues in your pocket, and feel free to use them as needed.

🙚 Check to make sure the microphone is turned on before talking. A little tap on the microphone will be projected if it's on and working. If the microphone squeaks or squeals, you are speaking too close to it. Adjust by moving your head away slightly, or if holding the microphone, move it away.

Before speaking, give yourself a few minutes of relaxation by going into another, less public room like the rest room.

🙚 Relieve excess stress by shaking each leg to draw nervous energy from your brain to the ground.

- Shake each arm and stretch your hands, as well.
- Work your face by opening and closing your mouth and making faces (here's where the privacy really helps!).
- Return to the public space refreshed and more relaxed.

This practice period offers the speaker and/or writer one final opportunity to sharpen or change minor elements of the eulogy. It's not the time, however, to scrap the entire eulogy and begin again. Having worked hard on writing the eulogy, the writer and speaker can have confidence that it's ready to be delivered to the gathered mourners. The mourners, in turn, will be generous with the speaker; they'll understand that it was written fairly quickly and is being read at a sensitive and stressful time. If the eulogist wants to distribute printed copies of the eulogy later, he or she always can do some revision first, as chapter 7 addresses.

Elements of Delivery Style for Maximum Effect

The speaker's delivery style itself can be enhanced by all of the practical tips outlined above. The most significant part of delivery, however, involves the voice and its projection. In this section, I'll briefly discuss and demonstrate basic vocal and physical elements:

- Pace
- Pitch
- Volume
- Rhythm
- Body language
- Eye contact

Pace

Pace involves whether you're talking slow or fast. As a rule, people can hear what is said fast, but they may not be able to think about it. The brain has to work to take what is heard and make it sensible. Especially when people are grieving, it can be hard to process words that are said too fast. Yet, many eulogy readers make the mistake of reading very fast. Often, that's because people who deliver eulogies may not be very experienced in public speaking—they're nervous and afraid to take too long at the podium. Even experienced readers might be nervous because of the high emotions that funeral and memorial ceremonies entail. But the fact is that the people in the audience support the reader and want to hear what is being said.

And so, it's important to *slow down*. How slow? This may be hard to believe, but what might feel too slow to you as the reader will probably feel just right to the listeners. Try not to read more than three double-spaced typed pages of 16-point font in fewer than two minutes.

Finally, remember that pauses can help the audience to understand that something especially important is coming up. You can pause longer between two sentences, for example, when one of those sentences says something memorable or tender or powerful that you'd like everyone to really hear and feel. If each sentence is spoken using its meaning and punctuation as guides, then the pace will be just about right for the audience.

Pitch

Pitch has to do with modulating the tone of your voice from high to low. Think about someone who speaks in monotone—for example, Ben Stein's television and commercial characters who talk using only one tone of voice. His voice drones on and we laugh because he never varies the pitch for a question, where the voice should rise a little at the end, and he never expresses excitement or any other tonal quality to vary the pitch. In the case of a eulogy, you'll need to avoid this monotone, and that means allowing yourself to use a range of tones *as they seem natural to what you're saying*. The key is to speak naturally and that will come only with familiarity with the eulogy, practicing aloud, and getting feedback from a trusted listener.

Volume

Volume is an issue of loudness and softness of voice. Just as nervous readers tend to read too quickly, they also tend to read too softly—as if they're afraid of being heard. Perhaps, at base, some speakers are afraid of being heard lest they make a mistake and have to begin a sentence again. As an experienced public speaker, I've had to do just that—roll back and begin a sentence again. No one minded but me. It's rare that someone will read too loudly, but it can happen. Try to have a sense of how the microphone, if you have one, is helping you project your voice. If you don't have a microphone, you'll have to speak more loudly than you would in most public situations. You need to reach the people in the back of the room as well as those in the front. This is a case when your "inside voice" is too soft.

Volume also should be modified at different points of the eulogy, and doing so can be helped with a microphone. There are times in the eulogy when you may want to soften your voice a little—but not too soft to be heard—such as when you read a poem or prayer for the deceased. On the other hand, when telling an exciting anecdote (like my brother skiing down the hill to the tune of the Olympics song), you may want to speak a little more loudly and with more animation.

Rhythm

Rhythm has to do with using the words and punctuation as guidance when speaking aloud. In chapter 7, I talk about rhythm in the sense of how words sound and how stylistic tools such as repetition and punctuation can vary that sound to create meaning in the eulogy. To establish and vary rhythm, it's important to be aware of how words, phrases, and sentences sound when put together. If you're a little unsure of what this means, pick up any young children's book and read it aloud. Usually, it's written with rhythm in mind. The eulogy also will have some of these elements, though not as many because it wasn't written for children but for a more mature audience. Using rhythm to deliver the eulogy includes pausing for emphasis, stressing rhyming sounds, and using a slightly different tone of voice to indicate other speakers, as with an anecdote that uses dialogue or a cited letter or poem.

> **Remember:** If at any point the audience appears to be distracted or out-of-touch with your message, you can bring their attention back to the eulogy by slightly changing the pace, pitch, volume, or rhythm.

Each of these vocal decisions can influence the eulogy's delivery. People who tend to read frequently or who are comfortable reading books aloud will find that these suggestions are somewhat commonsense and natural. Other speakers may want to practice with each tip, again seeking feedback. Preparation, practice, and delivery style lead to making the most of the eulogy writer's hard work.

Body Language

The speaker's *body language* during delivery also can influence how the audience receives the eulogy. Body language has to do with obvious things like posture and hand gestures, as well as with more subtle considerations like eye contact and head position.

People notice a speaker's posture—whether that person slouches or stands up straight is important because listeners make assumptions based on what they see. A slouching speaker might seem to be disinterested when, in fact, he or she merely is sad or nervous. Standing up straight, on the other hand, can be interpreted as being alert, ready, and eager to speak about the deceased. You might lean forward a bit as a way to indicate that you're a part of the group of mourners.

Hand gestures also tell a story. Presumably, when you deliver the eulogy, you'll be at a podium where you can rest your pages or notes. Your hands are then free to gently hold (not grip!) the sides of the podium, enabling you to turn pages as needed. Alternatively, you can put your hands at your sides with loose elbows. These postures and hand gestures are common among speakers.

In order to not call attention to yourself over the eulogy that you're delivering, *avoid the following postures and gestures:*

- Holding hands behind your back in the posture of a naughty child
- Folding hands in front as if reciting for a teacher
- Putting both hands in pockets and jingling coins or keys
- Fidgeting with a piece of paper or a pen
- Using frequent broad or expansive hand gestures

Eye Contact

Connection among the mourners is one primary reason for having the funeral or memorial ceremony in the first place. The eulogy further connects everyone by praising the deceased's virtues using stories that the audience will recognize. So, to come full circle, when a speaker makes eye contact with the audience, it connects them more completely with the speaker and the eulogy. Making eye contact doesn't mean that you need to look at every person; you can look to the left one time and to the right another time—or you can focus in the middle area of the audience each time. Making eye contact also doesn't mean that you need to memorize the entire eulogy. Occasional eye contact at key times is sufficient. For example, if you memorize the opening and closing sets of lines, you can speak them while looking at the audience. Then, you can return to the page to read. As you reach another significant juncture in the eulogy, you can signal that by making eye contact again. In fact, you can make eye contact with the listeners just about as often as you're able to with one caution: avoid head bobbing. When readers look up, speak, look down, read, look up, and speak again—that can looking like a chicken pecking for food. It's distracting. So, thoughtfully choose when you'll look at the audience.

> Delivering the eulogy is, in effect, your gift to the bereaved family and other gathered mourners.

The speaker's head position is part of making eye contact, especially in avoiding head bobbing. Generally, your head doesn't need to signal expressiveness for you as your voice is doing that job with pace, pitch, volume, and rhythm. However, there are times when you might use your head to help signal a turn in the speech. For example, when there is an interruption in a sentence like a parenthetical remark or a dash, you might tilt your head slightly or barely turn it to the side as ways of physically signaling the interruption. Then, your head can return to its normal position as the sentence resumes. Although you may not be aware of it, these are natural actions that people commonly do when they add an "aside" to what they're saying aloud. Similarly, when you use your voice to indicate that you are reciting a poem or anything that isn't your own words, then a slight change in head position might also be helpful to the audience.

Reading the eulogy isn't a dramatic performance. These delivery methods should be used judiciously. As a reader, you're not on stage, and people don't expect you to act for them. They truly want to hear the eulogy said clearly, audibly, thoughtfully, and lovingly. Practice your delivery until you're comfortable with it.

Speaking from Notes

Sometimes an experienced speaker is more comfortable speaking from talking points or notes. This kind of cued delivery requires a good bit of practice, but it will have a more spontaneous presentation than the delivery of a written eulogy. Most of the recommendations for delivery in this chapter also apply to speaking from notes. Nonetheless, I don't recommend it for most speakers during the funeral or memorial ceremony because this kind of delivery can be more stressful and, because there's a risk of rambling, the eulogy may be harder for the mourners to follow. Such extemporaneous speaking also leaves room for factual mistakes.

Truly "extemporaneous" delivery, by the way, is done without note cards or other cues. It might be practiced and rehearsed in some ways, but it requires a fairly experienced and confident speaker who has mentally organized the eulogy and has developed mnemonic cues for remembering that organization. However, if more experienced speakers want to speak extemporaneously, I recommend developing the eulogy's main points using the principles outlined in chapters 3 and 4, with attention to the stylistic concerns described in chapter 7.

Using the notes developed in chapter 3 and organized in chapter 4, speakers can make a set of note cards as cues. These cues can be complete sentences, but more often are bulleted talking points or phrases that remind the speaker of key ideas and when those ideas need transitions to other ideas. Using note cards allows the speaker to be more flexible in terms of the kinds of body language that this chapter has discussed. Head bobbing, however, can still be a problem if the speaker isn't very familiar with the notes. It's helpful to number the note cards in case they are dropped during delivery. In that case, it's fine to take a few seconds to pick them up, regain composure, and take up where the interruption occurred.

This chapter has illustrated key issues to be aware of when delivering a traditional eulogy that either is written or cued by notes. For the most part, you're now ready to deliver the eulogy that has been developed from earlier chapters. However, if you're interested in understanding the religious contexts for writing and delivering a eulogy, as well as ways that you might use this book to help you prepare a less traditional eulogy, chapter 8 covers those topics. If you're delivering a eulogy where the deceased is a child or children might want to participate in some way, chapter 6 will help.

Chapter 6

What Special Needs Do Children Have?

There are two distinct parts in this chapter regarding children. The first part addresses writing a eulogy for a child who has died. The second part offers supportive strategies for preparing children to speak publicly about the deceased and their grief.

Writing a Eulogy for a Deceased Child

Every person who dies is someone's child. Parents who have lost a child may feel that they have experienced the ultimate loss. It doesn't matter whether that child died in utero, as an infant or toddler, in pre-school or during other school years, or as an adult. When a child dies, a part of the parent dies too. The death of one's child simply isn't in the natural order of life. Our natural expectations are that the older person—the parent, grandparent, aunt, or uncle—will die before the child. But we know that while our expectations usually are met, there are tragically sad times when children die first.

When adults die, they typically have lived full lives and have had relationships with people in addition to parents: spouses, children, siblings, friends, co-workers. In these cases, although the deceased person's parents experience the unique grief of a parent for a child, the eulogy also can reflect that fuller relational life. All of the previous chapters of this book talk about that kind of eulogy. But when a child *who is still chronologically a child* dies, there are special needs that the eulogy writer needs to consider. While chapter 3 touched briefly on what might be written about a deceased child, the nature of children and the fact that they develop very quickly over the course of a few short years requires talking about eulogies for children in more detail.

How Children Die

Most children's deaths are accidental in nature. According to the Federal Interagency Forum on Child and Family Statistics, young children die more often of unintentional injuries than any other cause, including illness.[4] Falls, striking an object, or being struck by or against an object are the leading causes of death among children ages one to fourteen years old. As we might expect, younger children die more frequently from poisoning than older children and even these unintentional injuries occur more frequently than deaths from birth defects, pneumonia, and cancer. Children ages fifteen to nineteen years old are even more susceptible to death from injuries—up to 80% of adolescent deaths are from injuries due to automobile accidents, firearm homicides and suicides, as well as firearm accidents.

Because most children's deaths are caused by accidents, there's a lot of room for parents, friends, and other loved ones to experience feelings of guilt and anger. A need to blame someone or something for an unnecessary death can be mixed up with a family's sadness and general grief; left unresolved, such blaming grief can be harmful to the bereaved. Questions of "why" and self-blame often occur (for example, "Why did this happen?" "Why did I let him go out on a rainy night with his friends?" "Why did I hire such a young/old/inexperienced babysitter?") These are emotionally based questions that usually don't have clear answers. Those who've lost a child desperately need to ask such questions, but there's rarely a satisfying answer for them. In such cases, the eulogy can help the bereaved to heal.

---

[4] These statistics are for the year 2006 and can be found on the following two webpages; see (1) www.childstats.gov/americaschildren/phenviro6.asp for statistics regarding children ages 1-14 and (2) www.childstats.gov/americaschildren/phenviro7.asp for statistics regarding children ages 15-19.

What a Child's Eulogy Should Address

As we know, eulogies are written to praise, bless, and honor the dead. But they also function as an expressive part of the mourning process for the living. Eulogies help the living to confront the reality of the death and to express grief in the communal setting of a funeral or memorial ceremony (as well as in its afterlife as a shared or published document). A eulogy for a child does much the same thing, but it has the added function of expressing the family's and community's anguish about the hopes and dreams that are lost when a child dies. The eulogy for a child, therefore, may be more about these losses than the virtues and noble deeds of young people who haven't had the chance to fully form these parts of their characters.

Let's clarify that "child" in this chapter means anyone from a child who dies in utero to an adolescent in his or her late teen years. With such a wide range of ages and developmental stages, it's important to remember that there's no single rule for writing a child's eulogy because everyone's child is different. Nonetheless, there are some general guidelines to consider.

First, it's important for the eulogy to acknowledge the hopes and dreams that are lost with the child. In doing so, it verbalizes the uniqueness of the child and the family's vision for what that child might have done in life. Despite hard work and talent, the 9-year old ice skater will never go to the Olympics. Even though the 12-year old had an intense interest in biology and an aptitude for math, she will never become a bioengineer. The future soccer star, the handsome and sensitive adolescent, the child who wanted nothing more than to grow up and be a mother—all of these dreams die with the child. Such loss should be reflected by at least one to five sentences in the eulogy, as shown in the examples below.

Eulogy Statements on Lost Dreams and Hopes

We can't begin to measure the hole that Taylor's death is leaving in his family's life. He may have lived only ten days, but it takes only an instant to fall in love with such a beautiful baby—and we all loved him so quickly and so deeply that we can't imagine life without him.

~ Although Sara can never be a real doctor, we'll always remember how she loved to doctor her dolls and stuffed animals, making them feel "aw bettah."

~ Francis was just graduating, just ready to be launched into adult life. It's a tragedy that he'll never realize his dream of becoming a pastor. But even this tragedy pales when considered against the other roles he'll never play: college student, friend, husband, father, grandparent, and more. Most of all, he'll never delight his parents again with his soulful eyes and infectious laughter.

While such statements may seem too inflexibly honest in their messages, the loss of a child raises an awareness of death's own inflexibility: everyone—even the littlest child—will die sometime and not always at the "best" time or when expected. Those who are struggling with the need to fight denial and to acknowledge the reality of their loved one's death will appreciate an honest eulogy.

Second, the eulogy should acknowledge the family's anguish by making clear that the child is unique and irreplaceable. People fear that their deceased loved one won't be remembered after the funeral. While we may know in our minds that it isn't likely that a deceased child will be forgotten, in our hearts we worry that he or she will be forgotten in the world-at-large. In the eulogy, the child's uniqueness can be recognized by mentioning where he or she fits in family birth order and by addressing how siblings, in particular, related to this child. Interviewing siblings for a favorite memory can help with this goal. Another way to acknowledge the child's uniqueness is to tell one or two anecdotes—perhaps one from an earlier age and one from more recent times. These are ways to paint a verbal picture of the child and to assure the family that the child is irreplaceable and unforgettable.

When people cease to use the child's name—especially when talking to the immediate family—it seems like the child is being forgotten. The kind motivation behind this terrible practice is a desire to not bring up pain by mentioning the deceased; this motivation exists regardless of the deceased person's age. However, not hearing the beloved's name suggests the old adage "out of sight, out of mind." An example may help to understand this point. Recently, I spoke with a couple I've known for more than 25 years. Their only son Christopher died as a ten-year old 20 years earlier from a brain tumor. At the risk of upsetting them, I shared how much I learned from their brave fight for their son's life and their subsequent decision to continue to live their lives fully despite their grief. When I talked about Chris and used his name, both parents had tears in their eyes. Twenty years after Chris's death, it took only a few thoughtful words about their son to bring them to tears, but those tears were positive and healing as the couple expressed gratitude that I'd said their boy's name and shown them that he still mattered. The eulogy can do likewise by freely using the deceased's child's name and nicknames. Additionally, it can encourage the gathered mourners to talk to the family often about how and why they miss the child, which is another way of ensuring that the family knows their beloved child hasn't been forgotten.

Eulogy Statement Encouraging the Sharing of Memories for a Child

We know that Christopher's passing will always be a part of Ed, Diane and little Katie's lives. But they are a strong family that looks forward as well as behind them. They won't always think of Chris's death like they do today. Instead, in future years, they'll think more about his life: his joy at riding his bike, his playful teasing of his sister, his hard work in school, and his infinite patience with the indignities of hospital stays. Please, when you want to comfort this family, share your memories of Chris with Ed, Diane, and Katie. Let them know how you remember this brave little boy and tell them often that Chris's presence is missed. That's the best way you can honor Chris on this day and for all the days to come.

Third, some children have developed virtues and have had opportunities to behave nobly in their lives. If they have, then these virtues and noble actions should be shared in their eulogy, just as they would be in an adult's eulogy. However, keep in mind that some children die very young or at an undeveloped stage of their personalities and experiences. If the parents repeat variations of non-descriptive statements like "he was the best baby ever," "she hardly ever cried," or "his eyes were so beautiful and blue," then the situation probably is one of a somewhat unformed personality or set of experiences. In this case, as I suggested in chapter 3, it's a good idea to ask the family questions that are designed to learn what virtues the child has brought out *in the family* in his or her short time on earth. For example, you might ask:

- I know Bonnie was always giggling, toddling around, and getting into your pots and pans. What did you learn from being mommy to a baby in her "terrible twos"?
- How do you think Gregory helped you and John to be better parents or even better people?
- I know that Madison hardly ever cried. How did that make you feel? Did little Patrick notice his quiet baby sister? How did Patrick show that he cared for her?

The point here is that you may need to probe in order to understand what influence a child has had on his or her family. But even when there are problems or dysfunction in a household, people generally will identify some of the positive values that emerged just because that child was a part of the family. An example eulogy for six-year old Andrew L. can be found in appendix A.

Finally, it's useful to remember that every child's death brings its own challenges. As with adults, we're never fully prepared for the death even when we expect it because of illness. Since accidents cause the vast majority of children's deaths, everyone involved may experience deep shock and be somewhat inarticulate or filled with anger, guilt, or blame. In addition to the suggestions above, the following ideas may be helpful:

- Blessing or honoring the child can be especially healing, particularly in cases like automobile accidents, firearm deaths, and suicide. These are some of the cases where there's no good answer to the question "why." Poetry and song lyrics often can express what parents and other family members cannot yet say in their shock and pain. Be open to including the words of others in the eulogy and, when possible, encourage family members to be creative in the ways they memorialize their beloved child.

✻ In cases where it's obvious that one person or a careless event caused the child's death, it's tempting to point the finger at that person or event. It can be hard to avoid blaming and using angry words, but doing so is necessary for a healing eulogy. The eulogy isn't the time and the funeral or memorial service isn't the place to confront or accuse anyone or anything as the cause of the child's death. The time will come for such actions after the child has been laid to rest and the family has had time to deal with their initial shock and the first waves of grief.

✻ Similarly, the death of a child may become the impetus for the bereaved to protest some injustice around that death. Most readers will be familiar with Mothers Against Drunk Driving (MADD), which was organized by mothers who had lost children to the deadly mixture of alcohol and automobiles. Similarly, deaths that involve homicide, runaway children, kidnapped children, lack of safety controls in automobiles, and other product safety issues have provided the impetus for other organized efforts to make changes. Going on such a crusade may provide peace to some bereaved family members, but it won't do so for all. In fact, a mission to cause major changes in the world can become a substitute for, or enable family members to put off, the harder work of grieving their child's loss. That said, once again these activities and talk of them typically don't belong in the eulogy; they can be left to other, more appropriate discussions and venues after the funeral or memorial ceremony.

✻ Last but not least, whenever possible, the eulogy should include the thoughts and observations of all close family members. Siblings may have special needs that easily can be forgotten in the obviously crushing pain that parents feel. Because siblings often are peers in age, their experience of a brother or sister's death can be especially terrifying. All deaths are different, of course, but a sibling death demonstrates the real possibility that if one child can die—particularly in the unnatural order before the parents or grandparents—then other children, including siblings, also can die. This reality also becomes starkly clear when a child's schoolmate or best friend dies. In these cases, it's wise to find ways to include other children's voices in the funeral or memorial ceremony. Such ways are discussed in the following section.

Including Children's Voices

Children usually haven't experienced death often or they may not have experienced it on deeply personal levels. If they have experienced death before, children may have very strong reactions to being in a funeral home or church where a ceremony is taking place. When children do experience death on a personal level—such as the loss of a grandparent, parent, sibling, or friend—they often find it to be emotionally overwhelming. Depending on their ages at the time of the death, children may have pressing questions that range from where the deceased person's body goes to complex theological questions about afterlife. Additionally, children of all ages need adult supervision and protection from the most distraught (and temporarily unbalanced) grievers who might traumatize children in ways that can stunt their grieving processes. Children need to be introduced to the nature of funeral and memorial ceremonies by their parents or other caregivers. As the following information shows, the viewing part of the ceremony can be especially stressful.

Orienting Children to the Funeral or Memorial Ceremony Experience

> Funeral and memorial ceremonies can be confusing experiences for children of various ages.

For most children, the only experience they have had with viewings, funerals, and memorial services is what they have seen on television, in the movies, and in their video games. To help children of all ages, talk with them before they enter the viewing, funeral home, and funeral or memorial service. This conversation is the only way they'll know what to expect and what's expected of them. In addition, taking time to talk with the children gives them the opportunity to ask questions and express their worries and fears before attending the viewing or service.

In age-appropriate language, it's important to describe what the children may see, hear, and feel, as well as how they are to act. For example, you might say: "Many people will be dressed in dark clothing and speak in very soft voices. This shows respect for Grandpa and for all of us who are grieving. You may see and hear people crying loudly; you also may hear people laughing as they remember funny things Grandpa used to do." Many children and adolescents are upset and confused when they hear others laughing at such a solemn time, so this last point is important for them to understand.

Viewings can be particularly confusing for children and adolescents. For young children, you may need to describe what a casket is and its purpose. If the casket will be open during the viewing, children of all ages will benefit from knowing ahead of time what the body will look like ("There will be makeup on Grandpa's face to help give his skin the color it had when he was alive.") and how it will feel ("Grandpa's body is cold since his blood doesn't move around his body anymore to keep him warm. But that's ok, because when someone is dead they can't feel anything, so Grandpa doesn't feel cold."). Be sure to let the children know that the whole body is in the casket even if only the upper part of the casket is open. For older children and adolescents, the viewing can be especially difficult as they literally come face-to-face with death, a visual image that can trouble them for some time if they're not prepared for the experience.

It is not unusual for children to ask for information they need in ways that may startle an adult, such as: "Where are Daddy's legs? Can I see them?" "How did my sister get dressed if she can't move?" and "She's MY mommy! Why can't you make all these strangers go away?" Funeral directors, school counselors, and spiritual leaders are all people who can help you talk with the children in ways that will help them understand what is happening, why it is happening, and what the expectations are regarding the children. Let the children know how long they will be at the viewing or the length of the service. Also tell them how to behave—forgetting to do this can lead to some uncomfortable moments later when the children want to play hide-and-seek amongst the many floral arrangements.

Finally, it's also important to let the children know that over time they will feel better—that their grief won't always hurt this badly. Point out times they or others they know have overcome difficult circumstances. Children—actually people of all ages—need to know they will feel better over time. Ask the child what has helped him or her feel better in the past, and draw on those activities and experiences. If the child remembers how it felt when a pet died, that same experience can be used to help the child now. For example, you might point out to the child that he still remembers Frankie the cat, but he isn't as upset now as he was last year when Frankie died. Also, drawing a picture of Frankie helped then, so perhaps drawing a picture of his sister may help now.

Helping Children Use the Ceremony for Their Mourning

Children's needs to speak their grief can be honored in a variety of ways at the funeral or memorial ceremony. Children can be a vital part of the service by offering their unique perspectives, but they also can be distracting or even perceived as embarrassing if they don't have any guidance or age-appropriate boundaries. This section discusses supportive strategies for preparing children to speak publicly about the deceased and their grief.

When confronted with the death of loved ones, children may find themselves experiencing strong feelings that they don't know how to handle. For example, like the adults around them, children often feel deep sadness at the death of a grandparent. While such sadness can be a powerful emotion, most likely those people around the children will understand it. And, unless the children have been raised by the grandparent and have lost a true parent in him or her, then they may be able to see the grandparent's death as part of a natural progression; it's expected that older people will die before younger ones do. However, when the deceased is a child's parent or sibling, feelings of anger, guilt, or even terror may accompany the sadness. Indeed, as frightening and unbalancing as a parent's death can be, the death of a sibling (or a friend or schoolmate) can be especially terrifying since it presents the painful reality that if another child can die, so can the bereaved children left behind. In such cases, children confront their own mortality in ways that are common to their life stages.

Can or should a child eulogize a grandparent, parent, sibling, or friend? Recall that the traditional purposes of a eulogy are to praise, bless, and honor the deceased. Typically, I think of writing and delivering a eulogy as an adult's job because adults are cognitively more mature and better able to both think and write about a loved one's virtues and noble activities. While it would be a mistake to think that children aren't able to recognize virtue and nobility for what they are, the traditional eulogy especially requires a maturity of thought that children of most ages aren't prepared to offer. Children still need ways, however, to express their grief during funeral and memorial ceremonies. Rather than assigning them a portion of the eulogy, I suggest that children who express a desire to have a part in the services be given other, more age-appropriate options that don't replace or replicate the eulogy. Of course, there is no one rule for what's best in these cases and the advice provided here might not apply to your particular situation. But there are common-sense guidelines based on children's stages of emotional and cognitive development that can help adults and children make good decisions at difficult times. The rest of this chapter will focus on developing such age-appropriate mourning activities and how adults might assist children in this process.

> Immediate families of the deceased—both adults and children—typically do not take an active part in the ceremony because of the depth of emotion involved in their grief.

Infants and Toddlers

Infants and toddlers, of course, are too young to know intellectually what is happening in the case of a loved one's death, but if they are old enough to love, they are old enough to feel loss and grieve. Emotionally, they can experience their own grief, sadness, fear, and anger, as well as that expressed in their surroundings and transmitted through their caregivers'—usually parents—own feelings. Because infants and toddlers are preverbal in that they typically don't have the words to voice what they're feeling, they may express grief with inconsolable tears.

Children of this age have need of steady, loving caregivers to meet their physical and emotional needs during times of grief. Although babies' very presence can comfort their mothers and fathers, parents who are bereaved can help themselves and their babies by asking people that the little ones know and trust to stand by as babysitters and nurturers. Beyond that basic need, infants and toddlers have no traditional, active part in the funeral or memorial ceremony and should be subjected to as little disruption to their routines as possible.[5]

Preschool Children

Preschool children also are too young to be included as speakers in funeral or memorial ceremonies. Typically open to new ideas and excited by life, they are learning to take initiative. If they have been raised to believe in God, for example, they tend to use faith intuitively and enthusiastically. However, they project onto God (and any other powerful being) the good and the bad attributes of their own parents or primary caregivers. For example, if a parent is often angry, then their experience of God may be that of an angry, powerful being. Similarly, their experience of loving kindness and reasonable boundaries will suggest to them a God with these attributes. While they are verbal, preschool children still are very young in many areas of development. Under stress, they readily regress to expressing their fears and sadness with shy cringing, crying, screaming, lashing out, and even biting or hitting. At this age, children engage in a lot of magical thinking, which may lead them to see the death of a loved one as a result of their own anger, bad behavior, or unpleasant thoughts. Additionally, they don't understand death as an irreversible event and may ask questions like, "When will Grandpa wake up?"

Children of this age need focused kinds of support when grieving. While they shouldn't be speakers in the formal ceremony, they can be offered specific opportunities to express their grief in age-appropriate ways like

---

[5] Portions of this and the following descriptions of children's development and their responses to death are borrowed and adapted with the author's permission from Pat Fosarelli, MD's *Whatever You Do for the Least of These: Ministering to Ill and Dying Children and Their Families* (MO: Liguori, 2003). These descriptions are supplemented by the practical experiences of Susan L. Pahl, LCSW, a clinical therapist and elementary school counselor.

drawing and coloring a picture for the deceased and being allowed to place it in the casket or tape it to a wall for other mourners to share. They also can pick flowers to give to the deceased or to other grieving family members. However, under no circumstances should children be forced to go near the casket or offer a kiss to the deceased if they don't want to be there.

Other helpful activities for preschool children include:

- Drawing or coloring their feelings in a picture that they can keep (much like an older child might keep a journal)
- Picking flowers for the loved one's family
- Hearing stories about their loved one's delight in them
- Owning and/or displaying a picture of the loved one
- Lighting a candle for the loved one (with appropriate supervision)
- Dictating a message or having their thoughts written down by an older person
- Talking about their deceased loved one as often as they need

Elementary School Children

Developmentally, elementary school children tend to be concrete and literal thinkers. They become emotionally dedicated to their friends and classmates, who represent a world outside their immediate families. Generally, elementary-age children work hard and thrive on success, but their efforts and self-esteem decline when they see themselves fail. They are literal thinkers who gravitate toward mythic and super heroes. They have a strong sense of fairness and sharp verbal skills—and they may be somewhat graphic or impolite in their language, particularly when emotional. At this age, they interpret even symbolic statements somewhat literally. They ask concrete questions about God and attach blame to someone when death occurs: "Why did God take my Mommy away?" or "Did this happen because I was bad?" When children of this age cry in grief, it's appropriate to hand them a tissue and offer a hug. Their grief should never be minimized by platitudes or stopped by statements suggesting they're too big to cry. Tears are an appropriate response to death at every age. When these children ask questions like, "Why did Grandma die but Daddy didn't?" it's best simply to be available and present, giving age-appropriate information. Another way to be present and available is to acknowledge what the children might be feeling and then ask, "What do you think?" in order to understand better what their perception of this death is. Be open and honest in your answers to their questions and, if you don't know an answer, it's alright to say, "I don't know, but we will learn together." Acknowledging the thoughts and feelings of children gives them reassurance, even when you don't have all the answers.

At a funeral or memorial ceremony, elementary age children might express a desire to participate. Depending on the restrictions of the planned service, children of this age can participate in a variety of ways. For example, they may feel comfortable leading the mourners in a prayer that everyone knows, or they may be capable of reading a simple poem in honor of their loved one. In either case, children of this age need time to prepare before the service; the choice to lead a prayer, read a poem, or even choose a hymn for everyone to sing should not be sprung on them just before the service begins. They also need a sense of how much time their contribution will take so that they don't think they need to fill a perceived void in the ceremony. These children may benefit from the support of a caring non-family member such as a close family friend or their school counselor. In particular, some counselors will come to the home prior to services and then to the services in support of the involved children; these counselors often are trained to offer follow-up grief support when the children return to school.

Other helpful activities for elementary school children include:

- Drawing or coloring their feelings or memories of the deceased in a picture that they can keep (much like an older child might keep a journal)
- Standing alongside a caring adult who reads what the child has written
- Signing the guest book and adding a memory there
- Joining in singing a well-known song

> Using varied media like clay, Play Doh, watercolors, magazine pictures to create a memento or gift for themselves or for a grieving adult

Middle School Children

Middle school children are in their pre- and early-teen years. At these ages, children are becoming accustomed to greater independence and mobility. With their increased reasoning power and maturity, they are learning how to imagine themselves in someone else's situation. The new experiences they have in and outside of school teach them that the ways they've learned to look at situations aren't the only ways to view them. In fact, their childhood sense of certainty is rocked by the new situations that they notice around them. They have begun to need peer approval during this age. Middle school children understand that death is permanent, and in this permanence, they may experience a sense of anger or of being cheated when a loved one dies. Their perceptions of God in various religions are changing as they develop, and they may become angry at God in ways they wouldn't previously. In grieving the death of their loved one or friend, they have the capacity to both mourn the deceased person and to recognize the loss of that person's unfulfilled dreams. They understand that, with respect to the deceased, the future is irrevocably changed.

Children of this age may desire to participate more directly in a funeral or memorial service. While I believe that the eulogy itself should be written and delivered by a more mature person, these children may want their voices to be heard—particularly regarding the death of someone close. For example, they might want to speak a few words about the deceased. Adults can support them by helping them to choose one memory or experience, or even a poem and then rehearsing it with them. Regardless of the activity that middle school-aged children might choose for themselves, adult support and supervision is necessary. Adults should discuss with them the purpose and structure of the funeral or memorial service so that these children can understand reasons for any time limits imposed on their activity. Adult support also includes giving an okay to the subject matter of their activity. For example, if a schoolmate has died and children want to make a banner to honor their friend, an adult should make sure that the banner doesn't include potentially offensive material that may upset the grieving family. Finally, just as children should never be pushed toward a casket to "honor" the deceased, they shouldn't be forced or cajoled into saying anything publicly about the deceased. Shy children especially should be supported when they express the need to remain in the background at this traumatic time.

Other helpful activities for middle school children include:

- Delivering a few spoken sentences about the deceased, which are outlined or written on note cards
- Singing and/or writing a special song or playing it on the piano or guitar
- Taking charge of placing mementos like photographs or objects the deceased used around the funeral home
- Keeping a memento of the deceased (for example, shirt, pin, toy) and taking it to the ceremony to hold
- Creating signature boards for friends and loved ones to sign
- Writing a personal note of condolence to another bereaved family member or friend

High School Children

High school children are adolescents in their mid-to-late teen years. They have adult or near-adult level reasoning capability, but they don't always use it—particularly in exciting, dramatic, or frightening situations. Their emotions are hormonally charged, which may become evident in high and low mood extremes. Adolescents easily can imagine themselves in new situations and have separated themselves to some degree from their families. With their new identities developing, they have started to think more independently and to figure out what they believe, as opposed to clinging to the traditional beliefs they've learned in their families. Adolescents often express their independence by making many of their own choices, driving, and earning money. They understand the permanence of death; therefore, they may be spiritually angry or feel cheated by the death that they're grieving.

Because adolescents are so much closer to adults both in appearance and behavior, it may be tempting to ask them to present a eulogy for their loved one. My advice is to decide thoughtfully and in favor of the teen's most basic needs for support from adults. A traditional eulogy written and delivered by an adult still is appropriate, and adolescents are children who in many ways are inexperienced and unprepared for the emotions involved in writing and delivering a eulogy. For example, when children of this age have just lost a grandparent, parent, or sibling, they may be too closely affected by the death to participate in the ceremony as a speaker. There are times when it simply is best to be a mourner and to let others take charge of the ceremonial concerns. Bereaved families usually aren't active participants in the funeral or memorial ceremonies precisely because they are deeply bereaved.

That said, it may be helpful to some adolescent children to participate in a speaking opportunity particularly in such cases as when a friend or classmate has died. For example, one to three short eulogies can be offered by a few select teenagers. Adolescents can say amazingly insightful things that are healing for the deceased's parents and family. To best help bereaved adolescents interested in eulogizing their friends, certain means of support should be put into place:

- Adults should explain what a eulogy is and help adolescents to talk to their friends and peer group members about what virtues and noble deeds they see in their departed friends.

- Similarly, adolescent writers should be advised to think of one or two biographical stories about their friends that demonstrate positive characteristics—skipping anything that is potentially upsetting to the family like under-age or excessive alcohol consumption, unsafe driving habits, gambling, or sexual activities.

- There should be a specific time limit of about three to five minutes to help focus the talk.

- Before the ceremony, trusted adults should read what the adolescents have written—both silently and aloud to the teenagers so each can hear and revise, if necessary, the message.

- Adolescent speakers should be told when to expect to deliver this short eulogy during the ceremony and should know in advance where to stand and how to speak into a microphone, if one is used.

- An adult familiar with the speech should stand by and be ready to take over should adolescent speakers be overcome with grief and unable to finish talking. Other adults and friends should be available to comfort adolescent eulogists after they have finished speaking.

Other helpful activities for high school children include:

- Making a scrapbook or picture from materials like photos, newspaper clippings, and ribbons to illustrate their memories and those of others

- Singing or playing an instrument

- Creating an original song

- Recording memories/stories on tape recorder

- Cooking the deceased's favorite meal or desert and bringing to post-ceremony get-together

- Taking charge of finding or creating a website to post memories and photos of the deceased

- Finding a quiet corner and meditating for a few minutes— imagining they are someplace safe and comfortable like the beach or their own rooms

Many of these suggested activities for children at various developmental stages can be adapted to fit other ages. For example, both younger and older children can learn to meditate when they feel their grief become overwhelming. Holding such tangible objects as *Bead Blessings*, they can repeat helpful mantras like: "elephants never forget, and I don't have to either." Additionally, most creative media lend themselves to all ages for the purpose of representing the loved one or grief in symbolic ways. Music can touch most people in healing ways. When given the chance, most children—and adults, too—can be very creative in finding ways to participate in a funeral or memorial ceremony outside writing or delivering the eulogy itself.

Finally, it's useful to mention that physical activities, which are best done at home or away from the mourners at a formal ceremony, may be very helpful to children who are grieving and wanting to do something vigorous about it. Powerful emotions are best expressed, and children need a variety of ways to do this. For example, with a parent's help or permission, young children could put on a swimsuit and express their feelings by finger painting in the bathtub. Another physical activity for young children is to tape a large sheet of paper on the wall as a canvas or use large sheets of paper on a safe floor to provide an easily cleaned area where both negative and positive feelings can be expressed.

Additional physical activities include:

- Hitting a pillow
- Hammering nails into a board
- Exercising
- Playing a physical game like basketball or soccer
- Yelling in the shower or parked car (after letting others know)
- Kneading clay
- Scribbling on paper
- Tearing up scrap paper or old magazines

Chapter 7

How Do I Polish the Eulogy?

Once a eulogy has been written—or even after it has been delivered if time was very short—often it's useful to polish it. In this chapter, we'll look briefly at some ways to choose specific words and how to compose them in effective phrases, sentences, and paragraphs.

Please don't worry! This chapter isn't a repeat of high school English classes, where too many people learned to believe they couldn't write. There are different genres—or types—of writing, and the eulogy is a particularly forgiving type. I encourage you to put those old fears of writing aside. While never really helpful when it comes to writing, old fears are especially unproductive emotions during a period of grief and high stress.

This chapter begins by reviewing the audience, purpose, and occasion for a eulogy. Then, it offers guidance and support about style. Style involves using words gracefully and memorably. Since eulogies are meant to be spoken aloud, the words you choose and sentences you write can be especially powerful. There are four points of style that this chapter discusses:

- Clarity
- Appropriateness
- Energy

᠁ Creating meaning

By considering these points of style, you can write, revise, and publish a powerful eulogy that honors the deceased and speaks to the hearts of the audience.

Audience, Purpose, and Occasion

It's easier to make stylistic choices when you understand what a funeral or memorial ceremony audience might expect to hear given the eulogy's specific purposes and the occasion of the ceremony. To this end, the following paragraphs recap some of the most important points of chapters 1, 2, and 3.

Audience

Who listens to a eulogy or reads it later? The audience for a eulogy tends to be a mixed group. Many of the gathered people will be grieving for the deceased, while others may have accompanied their bereaved family, friend/s, or co-worker/s. However, the need for funeral rituals and memorial ceremonies is so basic to human experience—in that we all know someone who has died, is dying, or will die—that the eulogy most likely will touch everyone on some level. The audience members who will listen most closely probably will be family members. They will be listening for familiar qualities, characteristics, and actions of their deceased loved one, and they may be disappointed if they don't hear at least some of these things. Friends and co-workers also will be hoping to hear at least one commonly known quality or behavior of the deceased. Secretly, they'll hope to hear of a special connection between the deceased and themselves (or their group, if they are co-workers or members of a club or organization). Even for listeners who don't know the deceased and who are attending the funeral with someone who does, the eulogy still will hold their interest because they'll want to know something about the person whom their companions are grieving.

Purpose

The primary purposes of the eulogy are to praise, bless, or honor the dead, as well as to instill and uphold the values that the community holds in common. When deciding how to phrase your thoughts about the deceased, these goals lead to word choices that are somewhat more formal than those used in daily conversation. Additionally, it's helpful to remember that a powerful eulogy will include the family and community's highest values. Thus, having a sense of who will attend the funeral will help to determine how to express those values. For example, if the deceased was a strongly spiritual person who practiced in a specific faith community, then that community's values should be framed in words that the audience will recognize as part of their immediate spiritual culture.

Occasion

Thinking about the occasion for the eulogy also helps when considering style. The funeral or memorial ceremony provides a social space for shared mourning. For example, because the death of a loved one leads to grief, most people think of a funeral as a somber occasion. However, some people are naturally filled with good humor and are able to create healing laughter through the anecdotes they tell. Solemnity doesn't mean silence and it doesn't always mean somber words and emotions. In fact, tears often are accompanied by laughter. Thus, the occasion for the eulogy also may be a time for some lighthearted, respectful comments about the deceased and his or her actions. Joke telling, on the other hand, may offend family members and wouldn't be appropriate content for a eulogy.

Clarity

Clarity in a eulogy suggests that the speech itself be neither so short as to omit essential points nor so long as to become tortuous. This quality is best served through simple and direct statements. Thus, choose the fitting word when writing a eulogy. Writers need to consider three elements of clarity:

- Vocabulary that's geared to the audience
- Word choices
- Coherence

Let's take one element at a time.

Vocabulary

First, using *vocabulary that is geared to the audience* means that you'll want some idea of who will be attending. It's important to talk neither above people's heads nor below them. For example, in my father's eulogy, I chose some of the vocabulary to appeal to his peers, who also were professional people. Let's look at one excerpt:

Examining Vocabulary Choices for Specific Audiences

Many of you know that George lost three fingers to an <u>adolescent</u> injury, but most of you probably don't know how <u>profoundly</u> the accident influenced his life. With two complete hands, George would have fought for his country in Korea, a lost opportunity that always saddened him. So, instead, as an adult, George served his community as Cub Master, sports booster, and visionary for Parkville's <u>revitalization</u>. Professionally, George may have entered any one of several hands-on fields, such as contracting. But the loss of his fingers, though physically and <u>psychically</u> painful, led him to use his analytical mind and to put his love of building into drafting and, later, into engineering.

Because I was writing to a well-educated audience, I chose "adolescent" over "teenage," "profoundly" over "deeply," "revitalization" over "renewal," and "psychically" over "emotionally." However, if I hadn't known that so many professional people were attending the funeral ceremony, I might have made different choices. In retrospect, some of the simpler vocabulary choices—like "renewal" and "emotionally"—might have been better choices anyway because they would have a broader appeal for people who were deeply grieving and not processing words as they normally would.

Word Choices

Second, think about what *word choices* might resonate with the audience. Again, using the text above, words need to:

- *Be specific* so that the story you're telling or the virtue you're describing can be imagined fairly easily. For example, I used "two complete hands" rather than simply "hands" and "love of building" instead of "interests."

- *Be descriptive.* For example, using adjectives like "analytical mind" instead of simply "mind" or "brain" or "intellect" helps to describe an ability (to analyze problems) that's important to an engineer—and one that permeated my father's family life, too.

- *Convey the meaning you intend.* Doing so may require that you read portions of the eulogy to someone else while you're writing or that you use a Thesaurus to find just the right meaning (available on most word processing programs and on the Internet). Consider how different the following words are: "revitalization," "renewal," "regeneration," "rebirth," "restoration," and "repair." As the writer, it was my job to figure out which word would be best for describing my father's work toward helping a small town to become economically active again.

- *Convey action through the use of strong verbs.* Try to avoid forms of the verb "to be" (be, is, am, are, was, were, been, being). So, instead of saying that my father "*was* a Cub Master, sports booster, and visionary," I wrote that he "served the community" in these positions. I did this specifically because the verb "served" can be linked with the verb "fought" regarding the Korean War—"serving" is something that soldiers do, but it is also something that community members do. The idea I wanted to convey is that since my father couldn't serve the country as a soldier—something he had desired—he chose to serve the community as a leader.

- *Be brief without sacrificing meaning.* This isn't something that comes easily to me. I have to reread and revise extensively to get rid of wordiness in my writing. Think about the following sentences:

> *Original*: "As a professional worker, George may have worked in a hands-on field like that of a contractor, builder, or factory worker like his father."

> *Revised*: "Professionally, George may have entered any one of several hands-on fields, such as contracting."

The original sentence has 24 words to the revised sentence's 14 words. But I needed to carefully review the sentence to edit it for clarity. Reading the sentences aloud to yourself can help you figure out where to be brief, too.

Coherence

The third element of clarity is *Coherence*. Coherence refers to how well the different aspects of the eulogy fit together. It is developed through the use of *repetition* and *transitions*.

Repetition, which I also mention under "energy," is a wonderful way to call an image to mind or to reinforce a virtue or theme. Repetition highlights a concept or idea that the writer wants the audience to remember. The repetition can be used to connect different aspects of the eulogy, thus effectively creating a eulogy that is coherent. In a eulogy to Queen Elizabeth (Queen Elizabeth II's mother), the Archbishop of Canterbury, Dr. George Carey repeated the words "strength, dignity, and laughter." These three words appear together four times in the eulogy, and they are used separately, too. The words reinforce the Queen Mother's personal characteristics that the writer believed to be most memorable about her.

In the following example from Herb's revised eulogy, repetition is used at the beginning of sentences to link them. The key ideas are set out through the verbs "camped, fished, hiked, swam, canoed, boated, and water-skied." Then, using the repetition of "they" to underscore the family unit that Herb built through these activities, the ideas of canoeing and camping also are repeated so that listeners can understand how these activities taught Herb's children strength of character.

Using Strategic Repetition of Words, an Example from Herb's Revised Eulogy

Determined to raise his children as intellectually and physically adventurous people, Herb first taught himself the skills that he would then teach Bob and Susan. Bob wanted to learn to target shoot, so Herb learned skeet shooting first. Susan wanted to travel, so they took trips each summer and visited art museums on the weekend. They studied maps and read books about their destinations in order to make the most of their travels. In the style of a true Renaissance man, Herb demonstrated his deep love of science through his avid interaction with nature. Each year, he took his children to wilderness areas in Minnesota and surrounding states. They camped, fished, hiked, swam, canoed, boated, and water-skied. They canoed from Minnesota to the state's boundary waters. They did things the hard way so that Herb could teach Bob and Susan the strength of character they would need as adults. When they camped, they carried their own equipment on their backs, and when they canoed, they portaged their own canoes.

Similarly, *transitions* link ideas from one paragraph to another and from one sentence to another. They help listeners follow along and see connections among ideas. Useful transition words include "for example," "similarly," "however," "therefore," and "in addition." Many transitions are used in this book as ways to maintain coherence among ideas.[6] Grammar and style handbooks can be especially helpful in developing your writing style both for eulogies and other written genres.

Transitional Expressions That Can Bring Coherence to the Eulogy

- *Adding an idea:* also, in addition, further, furthermore, moreover
- *Contrasting:* however, nevertheless, nonetheless, on the other hand, in contrast, still, on the contrary, rather, conversely
- *Providing an alternative:* instead, alternatively, otherwise
- *Showing similarity:* similarly, likewise

---

[6] The transition words are cited from Ann Raimes, *Keys for Writers*, 3rd ed. (Boston: Houghton Mifflin, 2002), 27.

- *Showing order of time or order of ideas:* first, second, third, (and so on), then, next, later, subsequently, meanwhile, previously, finally
- *Showing result:* as a result, consequently, therefore, thus, hence, accordingly, for this reason
- *Affirming:* of course, in fact, certainly, obviously, to be sure, undoubtedly, indeed
- *Giving examples:* for example, for instance
- *Explaining:* in other words, that is
- *Adding an aside:* incidentally, by the way, besides
- *Summarizing:* in short, generally, overall, all in all, in conclusion

Appropriateness

Appropriateness includes the level of language that ranges between the highly formal words of poetry and the less formal words of every day speech. Appropriateness must be considered if the speaker is someone other than the writer. If so, the eulogist must think about whether the speaker will be comfortable with the language level when speaking in public.

Writers need to consider the following elements of appropriateness:

- Level of style (whether formal or informal)
- Stylistic choices
- Inclusive language

Again, let's take one element at a time.

Level of Style

First, a eulogy tends to be *more formal than informal* in terms of language use because a eulogy is given for a ritual or ceremonial occasion that marks a change in the lives of the bereaved. Second, the funeral or memorial ceremony is infused with formality that marks it as a ritual transition. For example, people may wear all black as tradition dictates or they may wear muted colors. People generally attend in their best clothes rather than work or casual clothes. There may be symbols in the room that indicate formal affiliation with the military or organizations like the scouts, Daughters of the Revolution, or Masons. These types of formalities suggest that the eulogy should be a formal speech.

Stylistic Choices

Seeing the eulogy as a formal speech can help you to decide whether to include colloquialisms, slang, jargon, and clichés. The single, most helpful guideline is to keep the audience in mind when making these word and phrase-based decisions. And, as chapter 3 explains, it's possible to personalize the eulogy for particular listeners by using the exact words that people offered when they talked about the deceased before you began to write the eulogy. These words might include less formal phrasings and, placed in the context of that person's relationship with the deceased, could be very appropriate. Using these exact words tends to resonate with the family and friends who provided the information and can lead them to think, "You've captured my mother exactly!"

Colloquialisms are words or phrases that crop up in common conversations. They might be signals of a locality like "y'all" from the American south or "howdy, ma'am" from the west, and they emerge when you use the word "sack" or "bag" or "tote." They also include phrases like "let the cat out of the bag" or "running around like a chicken with its head cut off." In essence, colloquialisms have an informal flavor, but that doesn't mean that a few well-placed ones shouldn't be used in a eulogy. They can create a sense of intimacy in the shared understanding of their meanings.

The idea is to use colloquialisms thoughtfully with respect to the audience and occasion. For example, I wrote in my brother's eulogy: "Mishaps that showed his humanness followed George <u>like ants to a picnic</u>." Of my Aunt Ruth, I wrote: "She could <u>knit in the dark</u>"; this phrase came directly from one of her sisters. The bereaved will recognize some of their loved one's attributes through the use of familiar colloquialisms. However, it wouldn't be wise to use a lot of American colloquialisms for an audience that has come from another country to attend the service; they might feel left out of the intimacy of the story because of not understanding the colloquialism.

Slang is the use of very informal words in nonstandard ways. It generally lowers the language level below what's considered appropriate in mixed gender, mixed age-group company. The word "ain't" used to be considered slang as a spoken form that means either "isn't" or "aren't." Remember when mom told us, "Ain't ain't in the dictionary"? Well, it is now. But while "ain't" may be used on television shows and in daily speech, it still isn't considered acceptable for formal speeches or in formal writing. Neither is explicit, profane, or vulgar language.

It's best overall to avoid using slang words in the eulogy. A reasonable exception may be a highly individual instance like using and explaining a non-offensive slang word in the context of a deceased teenager's life. For example, if a teenage boy liked to call himself a "hacker" because he was especially good at computer programming and addressed it with a spirit of playfulness and an attitude of excellence, using "hacker" and "hacker ethic" in the eulogy would be a creative way of both including the teen's friends in the mourning community and enlightening the older mourners about an aspect of his life.

Jargon is language that is used in particular activities, work settings, or other groups. It's shorthand language that only people in that group generally know. If you're a sports fan, you might be familiar with terms like "nickel" and "spiking," but if you aren't interested in sports, these words will have little meaning to you. Jargon isn't a good choice for a eulogy for two reasons. First, jargon tends to exclude mourners in the audience who don't have ties to the group whose language is being used. Second, if used incorrectly, it can disrupt the flow of the eulogy.

Finally, *clichés* are phrases that once had some interest or force to them, but have been so overused that they're relatively meaningless and even boring. "Let sleeping dogs lie" once expressed the wisdom of leaving creatures (or issues) alone when disturbing them would only bring trouble. Now, it is a routinely used phrase for simply ignoring a potential problem. Likewise, "we're all in the same boat" was at one time a new way of saying that everyone needs to work together because the result affects us all. The phrase is tired now, much overused in everyday situations. Where possible, avoid clichés in eulogies. Although not offensive like slang can be or exclusive like jargon, they tend to diminish the quality of the eulogy and easily can be replaced with more creative language.

Inclusive Language

These elements of appropriateness lead to a final piece of advice. Whenever possible, make the language you use in the eulogy *inclusive of the entire audience*. Try not to ignore the needs of the younger people who will be listening, but don't speak to them so exclusively that you miss out on the needs of elderly listeners. Also be inclusive in terms of gender. To speak only of male concerns, for instance, could alienate female listeners. The same goes for potentially sensitive issues like politics or religion. While it's fairly easy to leave politics out of a eulogy, religion may be harder since the eulogy may be part of a religious service intended to make connections between life on earth and an afterlife. But the eulogy, unlike a sermon or homily, isn't the vehicle for evangelizing the audience.

Energy

Creative language leads to energy in writing. You might think that you cannot possibly write something energetic in a eulogy. Not only are you sad and grieving, but the audience is as well. How could you write something peppy? A sense of energy isn't the same as pep. It comes from embellishments that make the writing come alive. Through the eulogy, the deceased is actualized—brought back to life through words and images. Stylistically, this concept means to bring the life of the deceased—his or her virtues and noble deeds and everyday existence—before the audience's eyes and ears. It means choosing details that describe, illustrate, and show the audience a person's life. It involves finding unique, but not "odd," ways of remembering the deceased.

Creating energy in the eulogy involves such strategies as:

- Metaphor and simile
- Personification
- Word order
- Repetition and sound

Let's take these elements of energy one at a time.

Metaphors and Similes

Metaphors and similes are common ways to make comparisons. You probably use them all the time without realizing it. Metaphors directly compare two subjects that don't seem to have any relationship. Metaphors usually use the verb "to be":

- Mary was a rose in bloom because of her mother's loving care.
- John was a storm cloud when he was angry.
- Jane was a lioness when her children were at risk.

Similes, on the other hand, use the words "like" or "as" to show similarities between two subjects:

- Mary was like a fish out of water when she played softball with her children.
- When he skydived, John was like a soaring eagle.
- Jane was as gentle as a dove in caring for her sick husband.

Metaphors and similes allow you to use language more poetically to make a point, and they can help establish a theme. They're not hard to create and, used sparingly, can leave a lingering image in the audience's minds. For example, in Herb's eulogy, I used an extended simile to compare him to the nucleus of a cell, as the example below shows:

Using Metaphors and Similes to Establish a Eulogy's Theme

- Like a nucleus that guides the genetic expression of a cell, Herb became a primary source of inspiration and energetic activity for his family and friends.
- Yes, as a nucleus, Herb certainly has guided the cell, which was the little world of people surrounding him.
- Then, in honor of this unique man, let us go out and be a nucleus to others as he so generously was for us.

Personification

Personification is another creative method for bringing a sense of energy to the eulogy by giving human qualities like speech, emotions, actions, or senses to an inanimate object or idea. As such, personification helps us understand the object or idea differently:

- Mary's stuffed teddy sits dejectedly on the piano, wishing she would play with him just one more time.
- John's bat waits by the door and hopes for another chance to hit the ball for him.
- Even the flowers have stopped blooming, sorrowfully refusing to sip from the rain in grief for Jane.

Personification is used in Ruth's eulogy to show the vital link between Ruth and her Bible. "Her Bible called her name and Ruth answered especially to "Proverbs," which was for her truly the 'Book of Wisdom.'" In giving the Bible the human ability to speak, the image is that of a book that talks to Ruth and guides her life, which leads to the main theme of the eulogy: "So it is appropriate here to see how this book of wisdom guided her life."

Word Order

Just as eulogies themselves need to have an organizational structure, the words within the sentences also need to be thoughtfully arranged. Many people think that the *word order* within sentences is dictated by a vaguely remembered sentence law: subject + verb + object. However, changing a sentence's word order is a simple strategy for creating energy in the eulogy. It's especially effective when you want to make a strong point or to create a sense of drama.

In my brother's eulogy, I told the story of our ill-fated toboggan ride down a Pennsylvania mountain. We walked up that mountain for what seemed, to my twelve year-old self, to be a very long time, while the ride down seemed to take just seconds. What I originally wrote was: "They hiked up the mountain in thigh-deep snow for a long, long time." In revision, to convey the drama of that adventure, I exaggerated the walk into "hours," used a strong verb ("trudged"), and reversed the sentence order of "they hiked up." The reverse word order of "up they trudged" has the effect of making the listeners think first of going up, which creates a sense of height. Using "in thigh-deep snow" last has the effect of making the trudging seem still more difficult. The sentence now reads: "Up they trudged for hours in thigh-deep snow."

> *Original*: They hiked up the mountain in thigh-deep snow for a long, long time.
> *Revised*: Up they trudged for hours in thigh-deep snow.

When you purposefully construct your word order in this way, be aware that word processing programs may wrongly fault you by underlining the words or phrases. Read your sentences aloud, decide if they say what you want, and ignore the software's auto-correct guidance when necessary.

Other examples of word order reversals are:

> *Original*: These many years later, we remember Ruth as a beloved, loving woman who lived a life for others.
> *Revised*: A beloved, loving woman who lived a life for others—that's how we remember Ruth these many years later.

> *Original*: Herb's life was one of adventure, intellectual hunger, and public service; and at the very end, he demonstrated noble self-sacrifice.
> *Revised*: At the very end of his life—one of adventure, intellectual hunger, and public service—Herb demonstrated noble self-sacrifice.

Feel free to experiment with word order whenever you want to make a dramatic or important statement. Once you've completed your new sentence, try reading it out loud to ensure it conveys the meaning you want the audience to hear. If your new word order makes the sentence feel awkward or sound odd, then try another arrangement.

Repetition and Sound

Of the various ways to bring energy to the eulogy, the *repetition of sounds* is one of the most musical when spoken aloud. How does repetition of sound work in a eulogy?

Internal rhyme such as we hear within lines of poetry can be cited as a part of the eulogy. Here is an example from Kahlil Gibran's "On Death." Notice that the repetition is not only of internal vowel sounds (shown by bolded vowels), but also of words (shown by underlines):

- If **you** wo**u**ld inde**e**d behold the spirit of <u>death</u>, open **your** h**ear**t wide unto the body of <u>life</u>.
- For <u>life</u> and de**a**th <u>are one</u>, even as the river and the **sea** <u>are one</u>.

Another way of using sound is the gentle repetition of consonants in the middle or end of words. "Pitter-patter" is an example of the repeated "tt" sound. Here is one line from my father's eulogy where the gentle repetition of the "h" and "wh" sounds are like a whisper: "Beth will never forget being her daddy's Gypsy, **wh**o **h**eld **h**er **h**and **wh**ile in pain from surgery...."

A third way of using sound is the repetition of consonant sounds at the beginning of words. Here are two examples from Kahlil Gibran's "On Pain," which is found in appendix B:

- "And you **w**ould **w**atch with serenity through the **w**inters of your grief."
- "For his **h**and, though **h**eavy and **h**ard, is guided by the tender **h**and of the Unseen...."

Creating Meaning

Being able to say what you mean clearly involves some understanding of the rules of grammar, sentence structure, and mechanics. Eulogy writers may worry most about correctness in these areas of style. Many of us remember school settings where we were chastised about grammar and mechanics. The happy news is that correctness, while helpful, simply isn't the most crucial matter in the spoken eulogy. The listening audience won't be sitting there with mental red pens ready to fix the speech.

To a degree, it won't matter if you have sentence fragments or run-on sentences *as long as* you can read those sentences aloud and their meaning is clear. Writing a eulogy that can be read aloud isn't about "right" and "wrong"; it's about using the best words for the meaning you want to convey. The importance of creating meaning is why you should have a good grammar and style handbook that you can refer to when you want to polish the eulogy—not because your former English teacher might see it.

At a minimum, correctness involves standard usage:

- Grammar
- Sentence structure and punctuation
- Mechanics like spelling and capitalization

Let's take these elements of creating meaning one at a time and apply them to the spoken eulogy—one that will be delivered orally instead of read silently by others.

Grammar

Grammar generally involves rules for sentences and the kinds of words that make up sentences like nouns, adjectives, verbs, adverbs, pronouns, articles, and so on. As this chapter has discussed, it's important to choose accurate nouns, descriptive adjectives, and strong, active verbs because they're powerful. Using verbs as one example of a grammatical element, let's see how different choices can enhance your eulogy.

Verbs are vital to creating a stylistically strong eulogy. Not only does a verb need to be action-oriented, but its tense needs to match your intentions. You may have heard that the entire eulogy, like a school essay, should be in the same tense. But that's not accurate. Simple rules for verb tenses are:

If you're talking about the deceased person's past life or life history, use the simple past tense: "John **played** especially hard when he **was** on our home team."

If you're talking about the family and friends sitting at the funeral or memorial ceremony—in other words, about the current day—use the simple present tense: "As we **join** together today, we **need** to remember that Mary is gone only in body—not in spirit."

If you're talking about how the bereaved family will grieve and feel the loss of the loved one in upcoming days, use the simple future tense: "Jane and her children **will experience** a lot of changes in the next few months. They **will need** your continuing support."

If you want to use verb tenses to help you cover all the aspects of time, then also use the "perfect" tenses. These tenses use what are called "auxiliary" (or "helping") verbs like various forms of the verbs "to be," "to have," "to do," and modals like "can," "may," "must," "ought," "shall," and "will."

If you want to show action that began in the past and continues into the present, use the present perfect (have/has + past tense verb): "John's son **has played** even harder since his father died."

If you want to show action that began in the past and was completed in the past before another action began, use the past perfect (had + past tense verb): "As we **had gathered** at Mary's house to support her family before this funeral, let us continue to support them in the days to come.

If you want to show action that will have been completed in a specified time in the future, use the future perfect (will + have + past tense): "When Christmas comes, we **will have mourned** Jane for many months, but in some ways, it may seem like only a few days."

Verbs also can be written so that they're expressing "active" or "passive" voice. Active voice gives the subject the action: "John **held** his mother's hand all day long." The passive voice is used when the sentence's subject receives the action and the doer of the action may not be named: "John's mother's hand **was held** all day long." A form of the verb "to be" and a past tense form of another verb create the passive voice. In this second example, we don't know who held John's mother's hand; it could have been John or his siblings. Perhaps it doesn't matter who did the hand holding as long as his mother's hand, indeed, had been held. When it does matter who did the action, a phrase is added at the end of the sentence beginning with "by" to indicate the actor: "John's mother's hand **was held** all day long **by** his sister Sara."

The difference between active and passive voice in a eulogy becomes important when you have to convey a difficult-to-comprehend action like suicide or the effects of an accident. One of the challenging things about writing a eulogy is making decisions about whether and how to express uncomfortable truths. For example, when my brother died, it was in an aircraft accident whose cause was unknown at that time. It could have been the fault of my brother or his co-pilot, or both, or neither. But even to appear to cast blame in the eulogy would have been inappropriate and likely inaccurate. I wondered whether I should say: "George died" or "George was killed." The first choice is active voice—George did the dying. The second choice is passive voice—the killing was done to George by something—the aircraft? the crash? fate?—and the doer of the killing is left for the audience to fill in. Which choice is best depends on the particular situation and the bereaved peoples' attitude toward the loss of their loved one. In this case, it seemed best to convey simply that George had died and to leave the way in which he had died unspoken as the audience shared the little knowledge we had at the time.

As you can see, choosing a verb or verb form can be very important to the meaning you are trying to convey. And, what is true with verbs also is true regarding nouns and other parts of speech. Being able to clearly convey what you mean is critical to your audience's needs as mourners. Because correctness can help to create clear meaning, it's wise to share the writing with others who are comfortable with grammatical elements and to use a handbook of grammar and style as needed. Having someone else read the eulogy before it is read aloud at the ceremony can help to avoid embarrassing situations.

Sentence Structure and Punctuation

Like grammatical elements, there are certain ways that sentences can be correctly or incorrectly written according to rules of style. Again, these rules are available in the common handbooks. We're most concerned in this book with how sentences flow for oral delivery, which will create the meaning for the audience. Sentence flow can be helped by writing in typical sentence patterns with occasional reversal of those patterns, as I discussed in the section about word order under "energy." One key to sentences that sound good when delivered aloud is the apt use of punctuation.

Punctuation for English language sentences includes the comma (,), the period (.), the semi-colon (;), the colon (:), the parentheses ( ) or brackets [ ], the dash (—), the exclamation point (!), the question mark (?), the apostrophe ('), and quotation marks (""). Let's look briefly at how these punctuation marks influence a sentence's structure and help make meaning.

While commas signal a short pause for the reader in that there are different clauses to read, the period signals a full stop in that the sentence has ended. The speaker takes a breath or simply makes a long pause before continuing with the next sentence. Of course, there are grammatical rules for these commas and periods, but the need for clarity in a eulogy outweighs the need for strict adherence to these rules.

Use of Commas and Periods as Signals to Pause or Fully Stop as Demonstrated in Ruth's Eulogy 1

Ruth was the third of eight children born to Madeline and John O. As the second daughter, her siblings believe she was her daddy's favorite. As the third child, however, she learned early on to care for her brothers and sisters, and she lived that spirit of caring all her life. Ruth was one of those rare people who grew up in a family of eight with all of her siblings remembering her fondly and with love. She was kind to her sisters Sherrill and Daryl and was best friends with her older sister Violet, who purposely failed first grade so they could go through school together. As a teen, she was friendly, fun to be around, and popular in high school.

In the example above from my Aunt Ruth's eulogy, all of the commas and periods are highlighted. Read the sentences aloud and hear where the punctuation asks you to pause or fully stop. Notice that sometimes the commas signal a new "complete sentence." For example, in "As the third child, however, she learned early on to care for her brothers and sisters, <u>and she lived that spirit of caring all her life</u>," the underlined portion is a second complete sentence. The reader needs to recognize that there is another sentence (and most people will) and read it with the full attention given to an individual sentence. Sometimes, the commas signal a list is coming up: "As a teen, she was friendly, fun to be around, and popular in high school." In this case, the reading will sound quite different because the list doesn't have repeated nouns (she) or complete verbs ("was fun" or "was popular") to make each clause a new sentence. Again, it's important to realize that commas can have different functions particularly as cues for reading aloud.

Similarly, the semi-colon can serve the same function as a period (which is to create a full stop) or as a comma (which is to indicate a list where commas appear internally in the list). How you use the semi-colon in a sentence depends to some degree on how you want the piece to be read either silently or aloud. A semi-colon typically signals to the reader that the two sentences express intimately connected ideas. In this next example from Ruth's eulogy, the semi-colons signal a full stop between connecting ideas. However, for anyone who reads it silently as you're doing in this book, the semi-colon should also signal that there's an intimate relationship between Ruth's daughter Colleen and the grandson, between Ruth's son Danny and the grandchildren, and between Ruth's son Kevin and his place in her heart. The semi-colon can be a fun, sophisticated punctuation mark; however, if you're uncomfortable using it, simply use the period.

Semi-Colon Use as Demonstrated in Ruth's Eulogy 2

Ruth's care for her children was well repaid. Her daughter Colleen followed Ruth's footsteps and became a practical nurse; she had a son who grew up knowing Ruth's kindness. Danny has made a living as a talented carpenter; he has two daughters and a son fortunate enough to have known their grandmother. And Kevin has made a living as a respected iron-worker in bridge construction; the youngest child, Kevin had his own special place in Ruth's heart.

The colon usually signals that either a list or another complete sentence will follow. I've used colons many times in this chapter for both of those purposes.

The parentheses and dash (my other favorite punctuation) have similar functions. They indicate a "parenthetical" comment, often called an "aside." Such a comment usually isn't a complete sentence, but a phrase of some importance to the message. These pieces of punctuation interrupt the sentence and the written material often is spoken with a slightly different tone of voice. In the next example, the dash interrupts the sentence with information that gives a clue as to how far a rural dweller might need to go to enjoy the simple pleasures and benefits of a yard sale.

Using the Dash and Exclamation Point as Demonstrated in Ruth's Eulogy 3

Ruth was clever in the ways she handled the near poverty that a pastor's family can experience. She made a sport of Saturday morning yard sales. She prepared for the sales the night before by writing down all the addresses she wanted to visit—some much more than an hour away from their rural, mountain home. She left at 6:00 AM with her companions as friends. Once they were at the yard sale, though, it was every woman for herself! She who found it, got it and neither friendship nor rank of any kind had any privileges.

Although there is an example above in Ruth's eulogy, the exclamation point should be used only rarely. Recall that it signals excitement and such excitement might be inappropriate in the text of the eulogy. Rare or not, the exclamation point has its own issues: how does the reader actually express it aloud? I discuss this concern in chapter 5 regarding delivering the eulogy. In sum, keep in mind that what you write likely will be read as it is punctuated.

The question mark is used in eulogies much as it would be in any piece of writing. It indicates that a question is being asked and it requires a slight rise to the voice at the end of the question—just as you'd do in everyday talk when you ask a question.

An apostrophe (') also is commonly used and easily recognizable. It shows possession within a sentence or phrase: "Ruth's care for her children was well repaid."

Finally, quotation marks ("XYZ") also help to create meaning as they show ownership regarding dialogue and cited poems and quotations for the eulogy. Particularly, quotation marks indicate that the reader might switch tone of voice for delivering these words, which tells the audience that they were spoken by someone other than the eulogist. For example, in telling a story about the deceased's friend, you might use dialogue or the deceased's own words, as I did for my brother:

Using Quotation Marks 1

Then, in the beginning of this month, he flew his new plane from Illinois. To use his own words, from a draft of an article that he wrote just last week about that trip: "My first landing attempt downwind was high and fast so I executed a go-around. My second attempt was dead-on. What a thrill! After I shut down the engine, my wife and daughter ran over to greet me. I did it! This was my first long cross-country in over five years and my first in an ultra-light. And while I flew the plane alone, I made the trip with all those who helped me plan, prepare, supply equipment, and think about and pray for me. Thank you all for your support."

Similarly, quotation marks create meaning by indicating that someone else wrote what is being cited, as with lines of a poem:

Using Quotation Marks 2

And so, as we mourn George and celebrate his life, let us not be angry with him for his love of speed and his love of flying, for those loves combined to make him who he was. Let us say, along with him, "Oh, I have slipped the surly bonds of earth, And danced the skies on laughter silvered wings." George, when you touch the face of God, please say hello to Him for us.

Mechanics

Similar to grammar, sentence structure, and punctuation, it might be helpful to review some of the rules of *mechanics* like *capitalization and spelling*. Today's word processing programs address the most obvious of errors in capitalization and punctuation. And when a capitalization error isn't caught, most often whoever is reading the eulogy silently or aloud will be able to understand a word or phrase anyway.

But spelling errors can cause problems in conveying meaning. Word processing programs typically won't catch problems that arise when a word is correctly spelled but is the wrong word. Take this edited sentence from Ruth's eulogy, for example:

Once they where at the yard sale, though, it was every women for herself!

There are two spelling errors in this sentence that could trip up a reader. Do you see them? Look at "where," which should have been "were" and at "women," which should have been "woman." These examples show a case where printing out the eulogy and reading it aloud very slowly can help to find potential problems. Remember that as writers, *we often read what we think is on the paper* or *what we wanted to say*. That's one reason that it's especially helpful to get another person to help by also reading the eulogy aloud from a printed copy.

Finally, correctness as an element of creating meaning may become more important to you in very formal eulogies and eulogies where the written form will be "published." Publication doesn't have to be in a magazine or newspaper, by the way. We actually publish our eulogies by passing them around in printed form, mailing or emailing them to family members, or placing them on memorial webpages or Facebook. At those times, being a little more "correct" is useful and can help avoid potential embarrassment.

If correctness isn't your strength, ask someone else to read the eulogy to find errors that might make the meaning less clear. Always proofread your writing by reading both silently and aloud before presenting it to the bereaved family. It's best to show primary family members the finished eulogy because they will appreciate a chance to approve the text and to check for any possible factual errors before it's read at the funeral or memorial service.

Because style—in terms of appropriateness, clarity, energy, and creating meaning among others—is a subject about which many books are written, this chapter has selectively condensed this subject to keep the writing process manageable for a stressful occasion like a funeral. There are quite a few easy-to-understand handbooks of style and grammar that can help you to check on words, phrases, sentences, and punctuation that you're not sure of. Your local bookstore or library should have some of these sources available.

Chapter 8

What Else Should I Know?

The bulk of *Good Words: Memorializing Through a Eulogy* addresses the traditional eulogy, which tends either to be written prior to the funeral service or delivered with notes as cues at the funeral. In either case, typically there is only one speaker. Knowing the basics of a traditional eulogy will help you to develop a powerful eulogy. However, knowing these basics also will assist you if you want to write a less traditional eulogy or to deliver it in more contemporary ways. When you know the "rules," so to speak, you can figure out how deviating from them can help or hinder a eulogy.

This final chapter addresses some of the special situations that eulogists may encounter. In it, we look at such situations as the various contexts for eulogies in different religious settings, writing the eulogy before a loved one's death, developing the eulogy for multiple speakers, engaging technology for non-traditional eulogies, and revising the eulogy after the funeral.

It's important to note, however, that some of the cases this chapter discusses are relative to particular groups, cultures, and geographic areas. Even the technology discussed is fluid and continually developing. Please read this chapter as simply providing some background knowledge and ideas that you should then review with the family of the deceased and the individuals presiding at the funeral or memorial ceremony. Doing so is especially critical when it comes to the practice of particular rituals in different religions because within each major religious group, there can be hundreds of different sects that have their own ritual practices and customs.

Understanding the Eulogy in Religious Settings

Eulogies are common in many cultures, religions, and nationalities. Even when they're delivered in a religious setting, however, the purpose of a eulogy generally is secular and not sacred in nature. Religious settings include a church or other consecrated or religiously designated building to include a temple, synagogue, or mosque. At times, religious settings can include funeral homes or graveside services. Secular settings generally are places like a funeral home, a private home, and a meeting hall or restaurant. In these secular settings, the bereaved can be fairly flexible in terms of whether, when, and how a eulogy is delivered.

In a religious setting, however, you can expect that the ceremony will be developed around a particular religious group's ritual practices and customs. For example, if the funeral ceremony is in a Roman Catholic Church, the ceremony will be conducted as a Requiem Vigil and/or a Mass. In this case, there are predetermined rituals and sacraments that a priest, deacon, or lay minister will enact. The bereaved family will experience the funeral Vigil and/or Mass as Catholics have experienced it for more than 1,500 years. By asking for such a religious service, the family is expressing that they want the traditions and sacraments of the Catholic Church. In this setting, it's inappropriate to ask for the priest or deacon to make changes to the ritual just to please the family or to follow the wishes of the deceased. Either the service is conducted ritually or it isn't conducted as a Catholic service. The same holds true for many Jewish, Muslim, Buddhist, and Hindu or Sikh religious sects. The more orthodox the group, the less flexible they'll be able to be regarding their rituals. This adherence to custom stems from the fact that formal religions are expressions of a broader, universalized (within that faith base) set of beliefs and they work because the congregations choose to worship under the umbrella of that faith base. Such customs are intended to support—not hurt—the bereaved.

It's important to understand the difference between a funeral or memorial ceremony that has a secular function and one that has a sacred function. If the function primarily is secular in that there is little or no religious ritual, rite, or sacred meaning connected to it, then the eulogy itself also will be considered secular.

Secular and Sacred Ceremonies

Secular ceremony:	→ Secular eulogy
Sacred ceremony:	→ Sacred eulogy
OR	
	→ Secular eulogy
OR	
	→ No eulogy

Quite likely, as a means of paying tribute to the deceased, the eulogy will be a major part of the ceremony. However, if the funeral or memorial ceremony primarily has a sacred function—to connect the deceased's life *and those of the mourners* to teachings about the nature of God and/or the afterlife—then a eulogy, if given, also may have a sacred function. Or, it may be allowed during or directly after the service, yet not be considered sacred in any way. Or, it may not be allowed within the scope of the religious service at all.

Eulogy writers need to know into which category the eulogy falls so they can understand the expectations of those who are planning the service. These expectations include:

- Whether a eulogy is allowed or encouraged
- When during the ceremony it is delivered
- How much time is provided for it

These expectations also provide a sense of whether the non-traditional eulogy forms that this chapter discusses can be part of the ceremony. It's likely that if a traditional eulogy isn't welcome, more non-traditional forms also won't be welcome for the ceremony. Of course, in such cases, based on the bereaved family's wishes and ability to host the mourners, both traditional and non-traditional eulogies can be scheduled for either before or after the ceremony.

The following is a very brief discussion of some of the major religious settings that you may encounter as you prepare a eulogy. Because this is a general discussion, it isn't possible to discuss all the possible iterations of the denominations and sects of these faith communities. Neither is it possible to be definitively correct in these generalizations. However, this basic background may help you to decide what questions to ask of a clergy person, funeral director, friend, or family member regarding whether, when, and how a eulogy fits into a particular ceremony. To learn more about etiquette at funeral services particular to various religions, read *The Perfect Stranger's Guide to Funerals and Grieving Practices*, edited by Stuart M. Matlins.[7]

Finally, as I indicated in chapter 1, our focus is on writing a eulogy that praises the virtuous qualities of the deceased rather than one that presents mere biographical sketches, exaggerated accounts of the deceased's goodness and accomplishments, résumés, or obituaries. This focus may create more good will with clergy of various religions, who may find them to be acceptable additions to their spiritually based services.

Protestant Christian

Although, of course, the funeral service varies among the many Protestant denominations, their followers generally are entitled to a Christian funeral service. This service could be offered in a church or funeral home. Often, it is preceded by a wake or viewing of the deceased. The viewing of the body is highly symbolic and an important way of understanding on a deeper level that this person has, indeed, died. Protestant church-based services tend to consist of appropriate hymns, scripture readings from the Bible and possible other sources, prayers, and some form of communion. Typically, there is a sermon in which the presider reaffirms the Christian belief in resurrection through Jesus Christ and, possibly, talks about how the deceased lived as a Christian. After the church service, usually there is a graveside service for the internment of the body or ashes. There may be an informal post-funeral gathering, as well. If the church service itself was private, the

---

[7] Woodstock, Vermont: Skylight Paths Publishing, 2005. Some parts of the discussions about various religions have been extrapolated from this book, as well as from *If I Should Die.co.uk*. http://www.ifishoulddie.co.uk/. Accessed September 9, 2008. Another excellent, yet more scholarly, text is *Death and Religion in a Changing World*, edited by Kathleen Garaces-Foley (NY: M.E. Sharpe, 2006).

family might choose to have a more public memorial service later; the eulogy may be delivered there, as well.

There may be one or more eulogies, which can be secular in nature, built into the order of the service. Individual pastors, however, may express a preference for a eulogy that connects the deceased's life to the belief in Christian resurrection. In some denominations, the eulogy is a cornerstone of the service. Because there are many Protestant denominations, it would be helpful to understand the particular values of the sect to which the deceased or bereaved family belongs. For example, in a Calvinist denomination, predetermination is stressed, whereas in Lutheran denominations, scripture alone is stressed, while in other denominations, good works are most highly valued. Understanding these different values can help in developing a eulogy that would resonate with the bereaved family and the mourning audience.

In cases where the presider will be including thoughts about the deceased in a sermon, it is useful to speak with him or her to provide specific memories of, or thoughts about, the deceased person. Doing so is especially important if the deceased wasn't a regular church attendee. It's embarrassing and saddening to the bereaved family to hear a pastor speak vaguely or incorrectly about the deceased. See appendix A for an example of a spiritually focused eulogy.

Catholic Christian

As indicated earlier in this chapter, the traditional Catholic funeral service is fairly stringent in its sacred rites. These funeral rites include three stages: the Vigil (or wake), the Requiem Mass, and the Committal of the Body/Burial; the family can choose to have some or all of these stages. Frequently, Catholics also have informal, post-funeral gatherings where sharing food cements the social connection around the deceased made at the funeral. Each part of the funeral rite has its rituals. The Vigil, for example, typically has a time for sharing stories of the deceased; the eulogy fits well into this structure and clergy often prefer it at this time. While there are some dioceses that practice funeral rites differently, they wouldn't be considered as offering the *traditional* rites. During the Requiem Mass, there are scripture readings, a homily that connects the readings to both the deceased and the Christian belief in the resurrection of the dead, Holy Communion, and interspersed hymns and prayers. The body receives a ritual blessing before it is removed from the church.

By Church law, a eulogy isn't part of the Catholic Requiem Mass. Sometimes, after the Communion rites and before the dismissal, a person may be invited to offer a few brief "words of remembrance," which do have a sacred function. In other cases, particularly when the priest doesn't know the deceased, a brief eulogy may be spoken before the Mass begins. These words, meant to take no more than about three minutes, are an opportunity for a family member or friend to speak to the deceased's Christian life and participation in the Church community. They are not intended for secular topics. One's human nature as a sinner can be part of this short statement precisely because the Catholic Church stresses that it is the human's nature as a sinner that both required Jesus Christ's sacrifice and an ongoing need for conversion of life. See appendix A for an example of words of remembrance. This isn't the time for a eulogy because, while a eulogy can bless the deceased, more often it's used to praise his or her virtues and noble actions. Such praise isn't in keeping with the sacred purposes of the Catholic funeral rites. That said, occasionally a pastor may allow a eulogy after communion as a courtesy to the bereaved family; in such cases, the eulogy may need to be approved by the presider. More often, however, the eulogy is encouraged during the wake or at the post-funeral gathering.

In cases where the priest will be including thoughts about the deceased in a homily and where no eulogy is allowed, it is helpful to speak with him to provide specific memories of or thoughts about the deceased person. Doing so is especially important if the deceased wasn't a regular church attendee.

Jewish

Jewish funeral rituals have their roots both in history and Jewish law. Although the rituals can differ among different communities, typically there are traditions that ask for particular actions and behaviors from immediate family members according to their places in the family. Because the bereaved family members have specific roles to play, they may not be able to acknowledge other mourners during the service, but would do so during the seven days of Shiva, when friends and extended family may call to console the bereaved. Whenever humanly possible, the deceased is buried in a cemetery within 24 hours of death. Both prior to and after burial, particular prayers like the Kaddish are said. Most are buried in a coffin because many Jewish sects view cremation as desecrating the body. It is considered both a responsibility and an honor to assist in shoveling dirt into the grave.

A eulogy, called a *hesped*, is a sacred and key part of the funeral prayer service and usually is delivered by the rabbi or a close friend of the deceased.[8] There may be more than one eulogy, which has both a teaching and redemptive function. First, the *hesped* teaches the mourning community by recounting the deceased's virtues and good deeds, which inspires others to behave well and repent of their own sins. As such, it incites people to emulate the deceased's good deeds. The eulogy enables mourners both to reminisce about the deceased and to explore the meaning of life and death. Additionally, the *hesped* can be seen as a spiritual pleading for the deceased before the Almighty— in effect, presenting a defense of the deceased's life. That said, as contemporary society becomes more secular in its thinking than in past centuries, it's likely that many Jewish services recognize the eulogy more in its secular function of praising the deceased's virtues and life than as a sacred act. An example of a eulogy for a Jewish ceremony can be found in appendix A.

Muslim

Eulogies are not part of Islam's funeral traditions, which have developed over several centuries and cultures. Services for both Shi'ite and Sunni Muslims tend to focus on burying the deceased within 24 hours of death whenever possible. Islamic belief is that the soul departs the body at the time of death. There are various sacred rites involved in the funeral, which include a ritual washing of the body, wrapping it in a white shroud, prayers for the deceased, and burying the body with the head facing the holy city of Makkah (Mecca).

---

[8] See "Understanding the Mitzvah of Hesped" by Yitzchak Kasdan. *Jewish Law Articles: Examining Halacha, Jewish Issues and Secular Law.* http://jlaw.com/Articles/underhesped.html. Accessed September 10, 2006.

Although eulogies are not part of a traditional Islamic funeral, they are part of some contemporary, secular customs. Thus, it's possible that a eulogy will be allowed in the settings of a funeral home, when one is used, and after-burial gatherings. In such cases, the eulogy writer will want to speak with family members, the funeral director, and the Imam about what would be appropriate material for the eulogy. Furthermore, it's useful to note that when the eulogy is moved to a secular setting, the eulogist can be one of a different culture or religious background. For example, in 2006 Prince Charles, the Prince of Wales, delivered a eulogy for a Zaki Badawi, a key Muslim leader in British society. Similarly, as long as faithful Muslims don't participate in the sacred rituals of other religions, they are able to deliver eulogies for the good of non-Muslims.

Buddhism

Commonly, Buddhists believe in reincarnation and that the soul is incarnated into a new existence as a fetus immediately after death. After many incarnations, the soul may enter *nirvana*, which liberates it from worldly trial and tribulation. Buddhism has well over 500 different sects whose beliefs and practices differ in small and larger ways, which makes it necessary to speak with a family member, funeral director, or presiding monk in order to know how the ceremony/s may be conducted. There may be as few as one ceremony or as many as three ceremonies involved in the funeral. A Buddhist's body typically is cremated.

As an example of the varieties of Buddhism, the Japanese Buddhist tradition consists of a funeral home ceremony with a eulogy and prayers; this service may last more than an hour. Cambodian, Thai, and Ceylonese Buddhists may have up to three ceremonies.[9] The point is that in the Buddhist religion, the eulogy again crosses cultural and national backgrounds. While its general purpose of praising, blessing, or honoring the deceased likely is similar to what I've discussed in this book, it's important to talk to the deceased's family. First, find out whether the eulogy, if it is desired, is sacred or secular in nature. Then,

---

[9] Stuart M. Matlins, ed. *The Perfect Stranger's Guide to Funerals and Grieving Practices: A Guide to Etiquette in Other People's Religious Ceremonies* (Woodstock, VT: Skylight Paths, 2000), 40.

learn where and when it's to be delivered. Its purpose and occasion, discussed in chapter 7, are key points for helping you to decide the content and style of the eulogy and how you'll deliver it.

Hinduism and Sikhism

The Hindu and the Sikh belief systems originate in India and are similar in terms of their common ties to the ancient Hindu religion. However, they have different core beliefs.

The Hindu typically believes in reincarnation and celebrates death as the means by which the soul can continue its journey toward nirvana or heaven, at which point the soul will achieve union with the one all-encompassing Soul, Brahman. The funeral ceremony can be quite lively and noisy as the celebration may involve horns and bells, welcomes flowers, and involves the eating of sweetmeats and other delicacies. Services may be held in a funeral home and involve scriptural readings and prayers. Cremation follows immediately with the eldest son or male pushing the crematory button. There may be a second ceremony involving the scattering of ashes. A post-funeral gathering of mourners is customary.

In the Sikh tradition, which developed by separating from the Hindu religion in the 15th century, there are different teachings and central scriptures that make up the body of its funeral traditions. Generally, Sikh's believe in a continuing life of the soul, which is reborn into human life as part of a journey from God and back to God again. Death isn't a cause for mourning in that sense, and so bereaved Sikhs tend to control their emotions. In this tradition, prayers are said and hymns are sung before, during, and after cremation. Post-funeral gatherings are customary.

As with the Buddhist religion, there are many different sects of the Hindu and Sikh religions. Some of these believers have left India and reside in other countries like the United States, which means they may long for their home country and customs at times of bereavement. It also means, however, that the eulogy, which may or may not have had a traditional place in their bereavement, has become more common to mourners and their ceremonies. Depending on the sect and/or family, a eulogy may be used during the funeral ceremony, at another time and place, or not at all. It seems especially important to talk to the deceased's family to learn whether the eulogy, if it is desired, is sacred or secular in nature and what its purpose would be for the deceased and the bereaved family. Then, upon learning where and when it's to be delivered, you can determine what needs to be said and how.

Humanism

Although there are many religions that cannot be discussed in the scope of this book— and I certainly don't mean to slight the faith of any reader—I want to end this brief discussion with a group that wouldn't designate itself as religious at all. Humanists, who would again involve many subgroups, don't believe in the rules or doctrine of organized religions. Instead, they follow a moral code that emphasizes reason and respect for other humans. They promote the attainment of happiness in this life because they don't have faith based around the supernatural or an afterlife. A purely humanist funeral ceremony doesn't include sacred rituals, and it easily can be adjusted to account for the bereaved family's personalized wishes. However, humanist services can become tricky when the deceased is a humanist but the family is more religiously oriented. In such cases, the services might be more spiritual in nature than the deceased would have chosen for him or herself. In the end, however, the funeral or memorial ceremony truly is *for* the living in honor *of* the dead. It is the family's right and responsibility to decide whether and how to honor any expressed wishes of the deceased as well as how to find their own comfort and solace in ritual. Often a reasonable compromise can be found.

When humanists have eulogies as tributes to the deceased person, there is always a secular function. A eulogy for a humanist ceremony certainly can be developed in the ways that this book describes. The keys to a good eulogy in this case are to talk with family members and friends for facts, anecdotes, and virtues; consider the audience, purpose, and occasion; and write and organize with all these in mind. Similar to other spiritually-based or secular groups, the advice in this book can guide you to an appropriate and powerful eulogy provided that you keep the specific needs and beliefs of the family members and other bereaved individuals in mind.

Writing a Eulogy Before a Loved One Dies

Sometimes a family has significant indications that a loved one will die. A prolonged or terminal illness may force the family to begin preparing for their loved one's upcoming death—although even preparation may not prevent the shock of loss and grief when death does occur. In these cases, especially in hospice and hospital settings, the entire family—including the sick person—is encouraged to work with and accept the inevitability of the death. In fact, some hospice assistance providers advise the dying and their families to write the eulogy as a way to prepare for death.

Writing a eulogy before a loved one dies has several advantages. First, the family has the time to develop a complete and polished eulogy that families who suffer a sudden loss rarely can do. In this case, I recommend reading the entire book before beginning to write (although jotting down ideas as they arise is a good idea). Second, the dying person has the chance to consider his or her life in the face of death, potentially contributing to the writing process and the eulogy overall. Hospice and other bereavement counselors can assist everyone in the family with this vital step. Third, and most important, this kind of eulogy writing provides a wonderful opportunity to celebrate the sick person's life before death or unconsciousness makes such sharing impossible. By allowing the loved one a chance to hear loving praise for his or her virtues and life choices, the pre-death eulogy can enable a special farewell and emotionally soothing moment for all involved. Writing and/or reading the eulogy with the sick family member can praise, bless, and honor the loved one and his or her family and friendships in especially loving and healing ways. The 2014 movie *The Fault in Our Stars* offers two exceptional examples of the pre-death eulogy and its power to convey love and appreciation.

Another scenario is that the deceased may have written his or her own eulogy before dying. However, before including this eulogy in the service, key family members and the designated speaker should review the deceased person's eulogy to see whether it's appropriate in its entirety and whether it would show the deceased in a reasonably good light. It's always possible to excerpt parts of the self-written eulogy into the primary eulogy or to share it in other ways. If the deceased person's writings pass scrutiny, I'd suggest that it be an accompaniment to a third-party eulogy rather than a replacement for it. As this book has stressed throughout, what others have to say about the deceased is part of the healing that a eulogy provides.

Including Multiple Speakers

Whereas a traditional eulogy is written for a single speaker to deliver, there are times when people want to write and deliver their good words using multiple speakers. Together, multiple ideas and voices can enhance the messages of praise, blessing, and honor that the traditional eulogy generally offers. However, without some kind of orchestration among the speakers or some guidance as to content, the multiple voices can deteriorate into a cacophony of repetition and vagueness. It's important to decide whether there will be one eulogy with multiple speakers or multiple eulogies. There are benefits to both choices, but challenges can arise. The following are some simple guidelines that can help with this decision.

First, a benefit to having *one eulogy and multiple speakers* is that the writer (or writers) has done the interviewing and is aware of what is going to be said. There will be no redundancy or surprises. If the writer has done well, the deceased's virtues and noble actions will be described with vivid anecdotes and strong, active verbs. The readers will merely have to decide who reads what parts. For example, one speaker can deliver the opening and part of the body and the second speaker can deliver the second half of the body and the conclusion. A challenge that emerges from this strategy, however, is that each reader needs to agree that the eulogy is complete and ready to be delivered. They may need to compromise or collaborate on parts of the eulogy. With two or more speakers, the needs of all have to be considered and addressed fairly—it isn't the time for egos to get in the way.

Second, a benefit to having *multiple eulogies with multiple writers* is that the deceased can be honored from different perspectives. The family can decide to focus on one virtue—say, their mother's generosity— while a dear friend could focus on her ongoing development as a loving person over fifty years of friendship, while coworkers could focus on her dependability. This scenario allows for the richness of the deceased person's best qualities to be spoken in the uniqueness of different voices. However, there is the potential for unnecessary repetition if the eulogists don't coordinate their efforts. Additionally, if a family member or close friend doesn't take responsibility for reviewing the eulogies ahead of time, the possibility of one eulogy being much stronger than the others could lead the audience to comparing them at the expense of the less gifted eulogist; in this case, the intended message may be lost. It's also useful to be aware of the amount of time provided for multiple eulogies. Some mourners will need to return to work after the services are completed and, unfortunately, may be watching the time rather than hearing the good words if they run too long. It's always important to balance the tribute to the deceased against the needs of the bereaved family and of the mourning audience.

Third, it isn't unusual to include *eulogy material that others have written*. Doing so includes another "speaker" without having that person co-deliver the eulogy. For example, many people recite poems or cite song lyrics in a eulogy to connect the deceased to broadly held or popular ideas. Similarly, sometimes the eulogist may want to use items that the deceased has written as part of the eulogy's content. This practice may help in conveying the depth of the deceased's being. Yet, some caution is necessary:

- The piece should fit into the eulogy as it is being developed—in the way that the excerpt from my brother's article about flying his plane from Illinois to Pennsylvania fit into his eulogy. If the context of the deceased person's writing doesn't fit, see whether it can be presented another way, such as part of a prayer card, handout, or program for mourners.

- The piece shouldn't convey bitterness, acrimony, or angry thoughts about anyone who might be attending the funeral or memorial ceremony. If for any reason it's necessary to share such writing, it can be done at another, more appropriate place and time.

- Any writing from the deceased should be reviewed by key family members before it's integrated into the eulogy or into the service overall. Getting their permission supersedes the wishes of the deceased as the ceremony is as much—or more—about healing for the bereaved as it is about honoring the deceased.

Finally, the family should think carefully about whether to invite *spontaneous remarks* from the audience during a formal funeral ritual or memorial ceremony. Doing so has become more common at contemporary ceremonies, and often it results in meaningful and special moments for the family. In fact, spontaneous, *informal eulogizing* is common at the wake, vigil, or post-ceremony gatherings. It's also common during home funerals where the body is laid out at the deceased's home and loved ones gather in intimate groups to say goodbye.

However, in more formal settings (including most funeral homes and churches) and particularly when the death is connected to difficult circumstances, it may be best to know what's going to be said—to have no surprises from speakers who could say unhelpful, inappropriate, or even hurtful things (unwittingly or on purpose). Inviting spontaneous remarks may lead to people putting themselves on the spot and feeling embarrassed or unable to convey their thoughts coherently. Worse, inviting spontaneous remarks may lead to learning that no one wants to speak at all, which is embarrassing for the family. To avoid such a situation, one might "set up" the "spontaneity" ahead of time by asking a few mourners whether they would feel comfortable speaking informally. Another option is to collect mourners' written thoughts and memories and share them in a separate ritual as part of the on-going mourning process. The formal funeral or memorial ceremony is only the beginning of the many ways we can use ritual and ceremony to memorialize our loved ones—as *More Good Words: Practical Activities for Mourning* discusses.

Eulogizing a Loved One Through Poetry

Grief never really goes away, but it becomes softer and less painful over time when we mourn our loved ones actively, as *More Good Words: Practical Activities for Mourning* explains. Writing poetry about our loved ones is a creative and soul-satisfying way to mourn the loss of someone whose death leaves a hole in our lives, and it easily can accompany or substitute for a eulogy when a later memorial service is held. While eulogies usually are written quickly because of necessity (given that funeral ceremonies typically happen within days of the death), poetry can take more time to percolate in the mind and soul of the writer. Like eulogies that are revised or written after an initial funeral to be shared with fellow mourners, however, poetry also can be shared in later memorial services or remembrance rituals, published more broadly, or it can be written solely for one's own satisfaction. The following is an example of a poem written years after a beloved brother died at the age of fifteen from cancer.

Eulogizing Through a Poem

Walking Quaker Whiteface Road I Meet My Brother
by Rosemary Winslow[10]

Yesterday a funeral, a bad X-ray,
futile the guessing—what future?
Heart turns backward, now ahead

now back again, tonight, walking the dirt road
that ends at the meetinghouse by the covered bridge
at the cemetery where the first settlers are buried,

when over the houses and pine-quilled sloped
a strange luminous fog opened around me
floating

the blue dark muscled onward
the sun not quite gone over
burning a bald rock face—bronze, red,

then amethyst, high over the thickening white—
too calm, I looked back,
a quick wind troubled my sleeves.

Once in my grief
I saw something of my brother appear
the night after the funeral

---

[10] Reprinted with permission from Rosemary Winslow, *Green Bodies* (Washington, D.C.: The Word Works, 2007), 11-13.

as I walked the floors of the house.
A place of whiteness, and sensed conveyance—
it is all right.

I am alright, I thought.
A president's funeral played on the TV,
Pictured of boys, brothers, husbands, my own,
In jungle fatigues washed out in static.

My brother, I said, not quite aloud,
so long it had been I'd spoken his name.

∞∞∞∞∞

You were a quick throw, baseball bat
in either hand, legs lean and fast.
You worked hard, played hard,

we walked the farm hand in hand,
kicked clumps of dirt, inhaled the richness.
What is it to lose a life you never

had time to live? I wonder now,
this thing in my chest, stone, or
lapsed piece of flesh over my heart.

That last night, all you'd been through,
trying to justify your unwanted arrival,
your life, then cancer, fifteen, the end.

What did you see when you said,
Everything is so beautiful . . . beautiful . . .
that vision you had as we stood around you

waiting, praying the night would not end,
your words continued in the rhythm of our breathing,
then you said—*Do you love . . .?*

It fell among us like an unfinished sentence.
My heart turned around on its muscle.
Right then I loved you mightily.

That is what you became.

∞∞∞∞∞

Reddening leaves of maples falling
into the gold birches
and onto the packed dirt road,

leaves scattering like melody
coming to rest,
my whole body was pulsing.

I got there in the darkness,
passed through that light filled fog,
went through the iron gate

which leaned open on loosened hinges.
Inside the stone fence the families' hands
had laid, who lay now in perfect quiet

next to each other, I stood a long time,
the day shorn, my feet hurting.
I was going toward death, maybe.

Yet I was happy. It was almost beyond beauty,
pine-fragrant, fog swirling the stillness,
the stones leaning, writing slowly vanishing.

I stood there. I stood, wondering, a clear space.
Michael, my angel, how are you?
Emptiness overhead hurtling the stars farther.

In Memoriam: Michael Kevin Landow

For those of us who aren't natural poets, *More Good Words: Practical Activities for Mourning* offers concrete ways to create and write poetry.

Engaging Technology for Non-Traditional Eulogies

Mailing, emailing, and hand-delivering print copies of the traditional eulogy are three common ways to publish and distribute it to mourners after it's been delivered orally at a funeral or memorial ceremony. However, new technologies have enabled a variety of ways not only to publish and distribute a traditional eulogy but also to prepare and deliver a non-traditional one. The following are a few of the innovations that technology offers to eulogists and bereaved families.

Digital printing offers an engaging and permanent way to deliver the eulogy while including photographs, poetry, and other scanned mementos of the deceased. Funeral and memorial ceremony directors have long invited the bereaved to contribute photo montages, poster boards, and memorabilia to the ceremony—all of which show the deceased in everyday and work activities with family, friends, and co-workers. With digital printing, these collected items can be digitized and organized into an inexpensive, yet nicely appointed hardbound book for a gift or permanent memento of the deceased. When the good words of a eulogy are added, they can deepen the meaning of the collection. One way to present the eulogy in such a non-traditional manner is to break it into sentences and phrases that encapsulate the theme of various photographs or mementos. To learn how to create them yourself, type "photo book" as a key word into a web browser; you'll be taken to a wide variety of companies that offer these services at reasonable prices.

Similarly, *digital video* is changing the way that individuals memorialize the deceased, providing media that can be viewed at the mourner's convenience. As part of their services, many funeral and memorial ceremony directors use the bereaved family's photographs and favorite music to develop video-based photo montages. These often are viewed at the funeral and are given on DVDs to family members as mementos of the deceased. Therefore, these DVDs offer another way to create a non-traditional eulogy in that if there is time, you can collaborate with the funeral staff to read the eulogy as a voice-over to the video montage. Another way to make use of digital video is to film yourself (or others) giving either a formal eulogy or a more spontaneous tribute to the deceased using video technology. These can then be posted via Internet-based "YouTube" technology to a website dedicated to the deceased or distributed via email. Of course, all the previously discussed cautions about appropriateness hold here, particularly because YouTube videos have a tendency to be shared widely and commented upon by viewers. To learn how to create them yourself, type "how to make a YouTube" as key words into a web browser; you'll be taken to websites that include free instructions for making and uploading these videos.

The Internet offers many avenues for honoring the deceased and distributing the eulogy. *Websites* are one such venue for memorializing a loved one. Some websites are sponsored by many funeral home services as part of the funeral or memorial package. Additionally, they can be developed privately by skilled family members or friends, although these will require some personal effort and may cost a nominal fee for retention on the web. One non-traditional way to eulogize the deceased on a website is to put the eulogy on a webpage and make it downloadable as a PDF document, which can be printed but not altered by readers. Of course, photographs and mementos that can be digitized also can be displayed on the website. Another way to invite collaborative memorials is develop a "wiki" on the website. A wiki is a shared writing space where people can contribute to the same document by adding, changing, and deleting from the original. The end product would be a more communal type of eulogy. Facebook, while not quite a wiki, is a popular communal web space for mourning and remembering the dead and for offering comfort to the bereaved. "Blogs," or web journals, also offer an interactive writing space where a single writer or group of writers can write about the deceased. People can respond to the blog entries using a "comments" function that is like the threaded discussion of a chat room or bulletin board. Teenagers tend to find these latter technological tools especially powerful ways of eulogizing a deceased loved one or friend because they both can make a statement and respond to what others have said.

Because technology changes so rapidly, no doubt readers will have heard of other ways to write and distribute both traditional and non-traditional eulogies. However, the major function of the eulogy doesn't change with the digital venue. It still exists to praise, bless, or honor the deceased and to help the bereaved family and friends to heal from the pain of losing their loved one. Regardless of the venue, these principles should guide what individuals say in their eulogies. If something wouldn't be considered appropriate by a wide variety of readers or if it would hurt the family, it shouldn't be written as part of a tribute to the deceased.

Revising the Eulogy After the Ceremony

When a eulogy touches them deeply, gathered mourners may ask to have a copy of it as a memento of the deceased or to share with someone who couldn't attend the funeral or memorial ceremony. As we know, a eulogy is written for oral delivery, and it's intended to be read aloud. However, as the examples throughout this book show, we often do share eulogies by printing them in books, mailing or emailing them, or publishing them on websites or in other memorial media. What can you do to get the eulogy ready for publication in print or online?

The first two steps involve planning on your part:

1.   Decide when you'd like to distribute the eulogy. Give yourself enough time so that you can do the quality of work you want to do. Most often, a eulogy has been written fairly quickly. Although there's been a great deal of planning for it in terms of talking with family and friends, writing and editing, and reading preparation, there's likely been little time for reflection and revision. Give yourself time but also a deadline—maybe one to three weeks if you want to distribute it broadly since the deceased will be on people's minds for a while. If you want to make a gift of your work for a major holiday like Christmas, Hanukah, or Mother's or Father's Day, then plan accordingly.

2.   Think about how the eulogy is to be distributed. Will you send it to mourners by email? Put it on a bereavement website designed for the deceased? Do you want to make a permanent hardcover book with the deceased's photographs, eulogy, obituary, and other mementos? How you decide to distribute the eulogy will make a difference in terms of the types of changes you want to make.

Once you've made your decision, you can consider the message the eulogy has conveyed. The best way to do this is using the same collaborative model that you've used in gathering information to begin with. Choose a few family members and friends to talk with; if you choose everyone, you'll be gathering this information for a long, long time. Ask questions dealing with the content, which is the first and most important issue.

- In terms of his or her values and noble deeds, has the deceased been fully and fairly represented?
- Does the eulogy's content reflect the person that you knew?
- Are there any stories or facts that should be adjusted for accuracy, changed, deleted, or added? If so, why and how?

Next, choose one or two people who you know to be good writers and ask them about the eulogy's organization. Keep in mind that the overall organization of the eulogy was a major decision and altering it also would be a major task. I recommend that you plan to make major organizational changes only if the eulogy truly needs it.

- Does the arrangement of major facts, stories, and values make sense? If not, what minor changes could help readers?
- Are there any changes in arrangement of sentences within paragraphs that could make the eulogy more clear and/or powerful?

Then, look at style. You may have needed to skip chapter 7 in order to meet your deadlines for the funeral or memorial ceremony. Now is a perfect time to rethink style because stylistic efforts will make the eulogy especially powerful. The elements of style that chapter 7 discusses are:

- Clarity
- Appropriateness
- Energy
- Creating meaning

Regarding style, keep in mind that the sentence structure and planned emphasis of a spoken eulogy can differ from that of a formally written document that's intended primarily for silent reading. When read silently in print form, a situation where oral delivery techniques no longer apply, certain sentences or phrases may "sound" hollow or less emphatic, or they may be simply "incorrect," which can distract readers from the message. This is your opportunity to work on those potential issues. If you don't feel qualified to do it, get some help from someone whose writing you admire.

Finally, when you're satisfied with the revised eulogy—keeping in mind your personal deadline—give yourself at least 24 hours away from it. When it comes to writing, the mind can do its best job with a short time away from the piece. Return to the eulogy refreshed and ready for a final reading—both silently and aloud from a printed page. Address any details where you see a need. Then, resolve that it is complete, finished, and ready for publication to the medium you've chosen.

Concluding Thoughts

Regardless of age, religion, or culture, the grief that the bereaved experience can either haunt them the rest of their lives or become incorporated into their lives in healthy, healing ways. There are many books and resources available to help the bereaved child or adult. This book's goal is to assist with writing and delivering a eulogy—traditional or non-traditional—that can help the bereaved to mourn in the social space of a funeral or memorial ceremony.

It's my sincere wish that all bereaved readers will avail themselves of grief support groups, grief self-help books, and experienced grief counselors as needed. We can be healthier and happier people—not to mention a healthier and happier society—by moving toward and embracing our inevitable grief and actively seeking to incorporate these experiences into our lives. Our ability to incorporate grief into our lives will also enable us to be kinder to other bereaved people.

Finally, as a eulogist, I hope you will congratulate yourself for doing a great kindness for the bereaved family. The gift that you've given them will last throughout their lifetimes. You've helped both them and yourself to heal and to incorporate this grief into your lives in a healthy, generous way.

Appendix A

Example Eulogies

I. Eulogy for George L., Sr.

March 5, 1936 – December 16, 2001

We are here today to say goodbye to George J. C. L.

All of you have known him in some capacity—personal, professional, or community- related—and all of you had a place in his big heart. To some of us he was family, to others a business associate, and to all he was a friend.

From modest beginnings, he shaped a life of great accomplishment. George, however, did not speak much about his beginnings and was similarly modest in professing his accomplishments. So, I will take a few moments to paint a portrait of a man whose life was full of accomplishments.

Born 65 short years ago in Brooklyn, New York, George was the son of Hungarian immigrants, Michael and Anna. With his sister Elizabeth, the family worked hard and soon moved to Philadelphia, Pennsylvania. Finally, the family settled into suburban life in Folsom, Pennsylvania. Together, father and son built a fine brick home adjacent to his Uncle Charles' property.

George's life and character took shape in Folsom. He was full of boyish pranks—getting scolded by his parents and having mild skirmishes with this sister. He worked hard and played even harder—most notably, he was an excellent pinochle player. George's integrity and single-minded purposefulness were a part of his being at an early age.

Many of you know that George lost three fingers to an adolescent injury, but most of you probably don't know how profoundly the accident influenced his life. With two complete hands, George would have fought for his country in Korea, a lost opportunity that always saddened him. So, instead, as an adult, George served his community as Cub Master, sports booster, and visionary for Parkville's revitalization. Professionally, George may have entered any one of several hands-on fields, such as contracting. But the loss of his fingers, though physically and psychically painful, led him to use his analytical mind and to put his love of building into drafting and, later, into engineering.

It was in Folsom, while attending Ridley Township Senior High School, that he met and eventually married Daryl, the love of his life. Soon George was in Baltimore, Maryland, with his new bride and a son on the way. Having moved to a new state and working on a new career, George and Daryl embarked on the life-long odyssey of raising a family. George, Jr., Beth, Michael, and Kathy were born in the span of seven years; raising them soon consumed both George and Daryl's lives. By today's standards of disposable marriages and late-in-life families, it is difficult to imagine the chutzpah necessary to start a family at age twenty while simultaneously starting a career and moving to a new city and state. This single mindedness was the hallmark of George's life.

George attended night school at Drexel Institute of Technology and later at Johns Hopkins University. He began his engineering career first with Glen L. Martin, and then Whitman, Requardt & Associates. George worked hard, studied harder, and became a Registered Professional electrical Engineer without the benefit of a college degree. He repeated that accomplishment in state after state, until he became certified in 11 states. After working successfully at Whitman's, George made a decision that would impact himself, his family, and many of you in this room. In 1972, with Ben Egerton and Maurice Bukawitz, he started E-B-L Engineers, Inc. Over the next 29 years, George and his partners developed E-B-L into an innovative firm that addresses electrical, mechanical, and fire protection engineering.

It is difficult to talk of George without talking about the firm. For some, this may seem odd, but for those who knew him, George's connection to the firm was natural. E-B-L Engineers represented the outward sign of George's life of accomplishments. It is neither serendipity nor coincidence that the "office" is a mile from his home and that we speak of him now a mile from his home and office. To George, the company was a life's creation—no less significant than his family or the rest of the world around him.

Speaking for the family, I can tell you that this deep connection was recognized early and accepted as part of his ambition and charm. And, although the family sometimes referred to the business as his "fifth child," they have come to recognize it as one of them. E-B-L will be sorely missed as a part of their lives. In fact, when the family learned that George had sold his interest and cut loose the last of his children, each had a similar response—that of surprise, confusion, and an odd sort of loss. Only George placed it in perspective and simply stated: "It was time to let it go and to move on with my life." Those of you here in business for yourself know how hard that decision is to make. Perhaps it will help you when you come to this juncture in your own careers to take heed of George's words, for there are lessons to be learned in this singe act of letting go.

When George died on Sunday, he was in his 46th year of a flourishing marriage that produced a life-long partnership and four children, who pursued their personal dreams. He never refused to support either his wife's goals or his children's regardless of how foreign a goal seems to him. His children married and among them produced six grandchildren, each of whom will miss their generous, loving "Pop Pop." Last year, George and Daryl lost their oldest son, George Jr., to an aircraft accident. From this tragic loss, George began to experience a rebirth of his internal sprit and a greater sensitivity to a non-working world. As the phoenix rose from the ashes, George, too, was being reborn as a man eager to explore retirement with his wife and remaining children.

George's children will each remember him differently:

- Beth will never forget being her daddy's Gypsy, who held her hand while in pain from surgery and who willingly provided advice and a listening ear as she struggled with various life decisions. Beth's wedding dance with her father mirrored many a childhood dance to the song "Scarlet Ribbons." Yet even as the dance symbolized a transition into marriage with her husband Paul, she knew she could always count on her daddy for unqualified love.

- Michael will remember the most unfaltering support given during his transition from self-employed contractor to an Architectural Conservator, MA. While his son naively embarked on the course of life change, George traveled with him, guiding him and often smoothing the way until he could stand back and applaud Michael's current destination. Michael will sorely miss his father's wisdom and never will forget the lessons he's learned.

- Kathy will always remember being George's Kitty Kat and spending countless hours with him repairing a car or landscaping the yard. Kathy and her husband Murphy will miss his smile and laugh—and occasional sarcastic comment, which always received a good-hearted "Shut up, George." Murphy will always cherish his friendship with George, which often took them to Pappas for oysters, beer, and a long talk.

- And Mary Ann, George Jr.'s wife and George's official third daughter, will always remember with love and gratitude his support during the bad times and his laughter during the good. She will sorely miss his wise counsel and hearty hugs. George's love and pride in his family was a lesson well learned by George Jr., and it has carried through to their children.

For Daryl, the loss of her life's partner is particularly profound. Together they withstood the pleasures and fears of raising a family, letting them go, and welcoming them back as adult children. They weathered financial challenges that would break many a contemporary marriage. They traveled, enjoyed life-long friend—such as many of you here today—and planned for a future unfettered by work and financial worry. Daryl led George to Compassionate Friends as a way to embrace and transcend the grief of losing their oldest son. Daryl stood by him as he and his sister buried their mother Anna this past October. Most recently, they had Thanksgiving with their entire extended family and enjoyed a relaxing weekend. Their plans for Christmas included a vacation at Ocean City with family and friends. So, for Daryl, this unexpected loss of her husband at this holy time of year is deeply painful. But, it is because of her love for George that she will have the support of family and friends, as well as the courage, to survive this loss.

In some ways, George seemed to believe that he would never die and he lived as if life would go on forever. But, that was just a façade. George planned for his death with financial support for his wife. He also thought about how he wanted to be remembered and it was not with maudlin songs and tearful stories. He requested a poem that his daughter Beth will read shortly. And he wanted his loves ones—all of you here—to celebrate his reunion with his own Father, the God whom he frequently called "Dad."

With great anticipation, George looked forward to one yearly event since moving his office to Parkville. Celebrating E-B-L's glowing success, the firm offers a yearly Open House. It has become the hallmark of the fall calendar and is a genuine throwback to the Bull and Oyster Roast that has made Baltimore famous. In the spirit of the E-B-L Open House, we'll meet at Jerry D's Catering Hall just a stone's throw from his office. And so, after the services, please join his family in celebrating the life of George J. C. L.

II. Eulogy for Herb P.

August 14, 1929 – October 27, 1993

Today we gather in memory of Herb, a man who lived life passionately with a thirst for knowledge, a zest for adventure, and a desire for public service. Like a nucleus that guides the genetic expression of a cell, Herb became a primary source of inspiration and energetic activity for his family and friends.

Born and raised in Baltimore, Maryland, Herb was the son of a civil engineer father and a homemaking mother. Although the family picnicked outdoors, Herb longed for much more. As a Boy Scout, he and his friend Jamie would frequently hop on a local bus and go to the country to collect rocks and minerals. He sorted and categorized the specimens, teaching himself the basic observational skills necessary in a future scientist. Herb not only completed his Ph.D. in biochemistry at Vanderbilt, but he engaged in learning throughout his entire life. His thirst for knowledge included reading all kinds of books and magazines about science, the Olympics, the arts, outdoors life, and more. He took art classes—dabbling in painting, sketching, drawing, and linoleum carving and printing. More important than the finished product was his desire simply to know more about how something was done. His curiosity and knowledge combined to make him a fascinating conversationalist—someone to talk with into the early morning hours over countless cups of tea.

Herb married for love, but his first marriage didn't work out in fairy tale style. When he and Laura separated, they decided that Herb would be the primary caregiver for Bob and Susan, their two children. And although the children spent time variously with both parents, Herb made the necessary adjustments to create a stable home for them. He learned to cook and set the habit of dining at the table while talking over the day's happenings. He stopped traveling as a grant reviewer for the National Institutes of Health, for whom he had studied cancer research grants, taking a less professionally satisfying position with the National Academy of Sciences. His sacrifices as a father came in the 1960s and 1970s when parenting more often fell to women than to men.

As a family man, Herb taught his children how to taste life. They ate strawberry short cake for Herb's birthday dinners and toasted s'mores over numerous camp fires. They developed a thirst and hunger for the best of what life could offer.

Determined to raise his children as intellectually and physically adventurous people, Herb first taught himself the skills that he would then teach Bob and Susan. Bob wanted to learn to target shoot, so Herb learned skeet shooting first. Susan wanted to travel, so they took trips each summer and visited art museums on the weekend. They studied maps and read books about their destinations in order to make the most of their travels. In the style of a true Renaissance man, Herb demonstrated his deep love of science through his avid interaction with nature. Each year, he took his children to wilderness areas in Minnesota and surrounding states. They camped, fished, hiked, swam, canoed, boated, and water-skied. They canoed from Minnesota to the state's boundary waters. They did things the hard way so that Herb could teach Bob and Susan the strength of character they would need as adults. When they camped, they carried their own equipment on their backs, and when they canoed, they portaged their own canoes.

As a father, Herb taught his children to look at the world both scientifically and creatively, in a way that led both brother and sister to revere nature and to seek out others who love it as well. Bob remains an avid fisherman and rock climber. Susan camps, hikes, scuba dives, and takes every class she can about drumming, the Native American flute, and folk art. She shares these interests with her husband Rick. Herb's legacy has been passed down to some of his grandchildren who have sought out a relationship with nature in their own lives. His granddaughter Dawn, herself an artist, is an avid photographer, diver, and bicyclist. Even I discovered my love of the water and learned to swim from Susan, who generously shared her father with me when we were roommates in college. In fact, he treated us equally as daughters, giving us identical jade bracelets for our graduations. When my own son Russ was six, Herb gave him a book on astronomy. From this treasured guidebook, Russ steered his own Ph.D. studies to the unique area of computer science as applied to astrophysics. Yes, as a nucleus, Herb certainly has guided the cell, which was the little world of people surrounding him.

There's no doubt that Herb loved his children. For example, he supported Susan's decision to divorce her first husband when doing so became necessary. Because she was a single mother and he so revered the needs of family, Herb set aside his intense need for privacy and welcomed her back into his home. He gave up his living room and dining room so that Susan could create a family day care facility that allowed her to stay at home and raise her daughter Dawn while earning enough money to contribute to the household and save for graduate school. A few years later, when she was on her feet and in her own apartment, Susan became sick. Herb gladly came to her home and settled in to care for her and Dawn until she was well.

Although unlucky in love with his first and second wife, Herb found the love of his life in Polly. They had dated at one time and reluctantly decided to part ways as Herb was not yet ready for marriage. Seventeen years later, when they saw each other again across the lobby of the Kennedy Center, they reconnected and became inseparable. During the illness that took his life, Polly cared for Herb honorably. It can never be said that anyone took better care of a beloved husband than Polly did for Herb.

In his final working years, Herb worked for the National Cancer Institute. He believed in its cause. His generous life of public service was one reason that his daughter Susan would become a licensed clinical social worker and later an elementary school counselor. Ironically, given Herb's public service as a scientist in the cause of studying cancer, cancer took his life at the youthful age of sixty-three. Yet, even as non-Hodgkin's Lymphoma destroyed his body, Herb maintained his love for life. He greatly enjoyed his Dawn, then a third grade newbie in clarinet playing, as she played scales and songs for him whenever possible. He delighted in the fact that Rick had refurbished Herb's thirty-year-old Boston Whaler and took him, Polly, and Susan for a leisurely cruise up and down the Potomac River—a final ride on the water. And, shortly before he died, he lovingly reconnected with his estranged son Bob on an early fall day in his beloved countryside.

At the very end of his life—one of adventure, intellectual hunger, and public service— Herb demonstrated noble self-sacrifice. Ravaged by cancer, he was aware that he looked sick—"awful" was the way he put it. He wanted desperately to go to his apartment's pool to paddle about in the buoyant freedom of the water. Polly was happy to take him, but Herb declined. He believed that he would look too scary to any children who might be there. His thoughts were for others, not himself.

In closing, let us sit in silent memory of Herb who taught us so much and guided us so well. Then, in honor of this unique man, let us go out and be a nucleus to others as he so generously was for us.

III. Eulogy for Catherine "Kitty" H.

January 2, 1927 – July 15, 2002

Today we gather to mourn our loss of Catherine—affectionately known to everyone as "Kitty." She leaves behind a loving husband of 52 years, three married children, and eight grandchildren. But we who loved her are not the measure of Kitty's life. No, the measure of her life is in how she lived out her life's guiding principles. Kitty's guiding principles were to honor God, to take care of her family and herself, and to give to the communities in which she lived.

Kitty grew up in an Italian Catholic family, where devotion to God was a primary responsibility. She learned early that prayer, going to Mass, and loving and caring for others were values and actions that any Christian woman should practice. Kitty often went to weekday Mass and read Scripture daily. Because her parents were divorced, Kitty's family was somewhat unique for the first half of the twentieth century. She and her siblings gave their loyalty to their mother, and they put their energies into helping the family succeed. They worked hard in support of each other and their mother.

Like many women of Kitty's era, her life's adventures began after high school with a job. She worked in the purchasing department for Dupont in Wilmington. Through a co- worker, she met Paul, who worked in Dupont's engineering department. She was lovely and chic; he was handsome and suave, a big band trombone player who swept her off her feet. They married in May, 1950 and joined their lives for better and for worse. Together, they practiced their deep Catholic faith and imagined all the wonderful experiences that God had in store for them in their future.

Five short months after their marriage, Paul was called to active duty in the Army, and Kitty became an Army officer's wife. It wasn't an easy life, but she was highly adaptable and eager to support Paul in his career as an Army officer. She quickly learned how to socialize and work with other officers' wives, some of whom had come from more privileged backgrounds and had more experience with the military. And she adjusted.

Military life can be unpredictable, hard, and exciting for the adventurous soul. When children came along, Kitty became a surrogate father during separations while Paul variably went to Korea, Vietnam, and other unnamed places. While separated—as every military spouse knows—there were numerous equipment breakdowns; it seemed like household machines and appliances waited for Paul's absence to stop working. Kitty was called on to figure out how to fix everything from washing machines to lawn mowers. It seemed that the children's biggest illnesses occurred during separations, too: chicken pox, measles, high fevers, and tonsillitis. Kitty proved herself up to these challenges because love of her family was second only to her love of God.

During some years, Paul's absences and odd work hours required that Kitty single-handedly raise Paul, Jr., Bill, and Camie. Bill sees this act as one of supreme nobility—in a time when women were being told that keeping a home and raising a family were a waste of talents, Kitty understood the primary importance of her work as wife and mother. She instilled values in the children that they would need in their lives. Going to church to worship was a primary value that was assisted by sending the children to parochial schools for as much of their education as possible. In these schools, they excelled and experienced the opportunity to discuss and practice moral and ethical living. Since raising the children on an Army officer's pay in the 1960s and 1970s wasn't easy, Kitty went to work to help pay for private school and other necessities. She taught them to love books and reading, buying books and taking them to the library. She taught them to cook, do laundry, iron, sew hems and buttons, and to shop economically for food. When her own mother needed daily assistance, Kitty and Paul welcomed her into their home. The entire family learned how important it is to lovingly welcome and care for others in need. In short, Kitty prepared her children for life outside her home. Her goal was to raise mature, independent children who would make their own ways in life. In this goal, she certainly succeeded.

Paul, Jr. and his wife Beth had one son, Russ. Bill and his wife Tammy had two sons, Daniel and Nathan, and a daughter Chloe. Camie and her husband Chris had a son Nikolas and a daughter Caitlind. Together with Bill's first daughter Melissa and Camie's stepdaughter Chrislynn, Kitty never missed an opportunity to lavish love on all these grandchildren. They remember going to the beach with her and walking the Rehoboth boardwalk. They rode the kiddie rides together—not much of a problem for Kitty's 4'11" frame. When the grandchildren visited their Delaware home, Kitty engaged them in walks around the neighborhood, crabbing, fishing, gardening, raking leaves, and shopping for sweet corn and watermelon. Daniel especially remembers going on his first Volksmarch with his grandparents—he was amazed at how far 10 kilometers was and Kitty really encouraged him to stretch his then-short legs. Together they shared the pleasures of an after-walk snack of a bratwurst and a drink. The grandchildren remember happy birthday cards, special hugs and kisses, and Christmas raviolis; the boys especially enjoyed their years of seeing how many raviolis they could eat without bursting. The grandchildren were treated to Kitty's aphorisms just like their parents before them: "You're sad? Well, you'll just have to get glad again!" "Do your best and it'll be good enough," and "It'll all work out in the end." She wanted all her grandchildren to learn that life may not be easy, but it is good and our attitudes can make it even better.

No woman can live long and happily if she doesn't take care of herself. Wisely, Kitty also gave to herself. She liked to be active by swimming, bowling, aquasizing, and walking. Kitty and Paul were especially happy when they participated in Volksmarching, a German walking sport that Americans have adopted. Paul, Jr., Beth, and Russ took them on their very first Volksmarch in Frankfurt, Germany. Kitty and Paul fell in love with the sport and, as members of the American Volkssport Association, they walked at least 10 kilometers in each of our country's fifty states, as well as in Canada, Mexico, and some countries in Europe—an achievement of which Kitty was especially proud. She liked to keep her mind and hands busy, too. An avid reader, the books that Kitty loved were passed among the family and outside to friends. She learned to sew, needlepoint, paint and fire pottery, and hook rugs; and she used these items to decorate her spotlessly clean house.

Perhaps Kitty's favorite pastime was to travel. Warm and quick to laugh, she could easily transcend the challenges of languages, and she made friends wherever she traveled. During Paul's military career, Kitty lived in both Heidelberg and West Berlin, Germany; as a family, they traveled to Rome and to the small town of Trisungo, Italy from which Kitty's family had emigrated. There, the town's people were so excited to have her visit that they asked Kitty to get out of the car and walk into the village in a spontaneous parade that honored her return. The family was wined and dined, making for unforgettable memories for each of the children. Years later, when Paul, Jr. and Bill entered the military, Kitty was able to go to the Azores to see Bill's newborn son and to Nurnberg, Germany to visit with Paul, Jr. shortly before his son was born. The highlight of her many travels with Paul was an inspiring visit to the Holy Land, where she experienced a renewal of faith that carried her throughout her last years.

Within each of Kitty's homes—and there were at least a dozen house changes during Kitty's life with Paul—she became an avid part of the community. At church, Kitty was a Eucharistic Minister so that she could offer Holy Communion to shut-ins and the sick. She and Paul conducted RCIA classes, which teach people who want to convert to Catholicism. She was active on a prayer line and kept an on-going list to pray for those who were in need of love, support, and help. Kitty's neighbors and friends always knew that she would be there for them. She had an unusually powerful ability to express love openly and was known to drop her plans immediately to be with someone in need. Whether it was her own children or people in her neighborhood, Kitty flew, drove, or walked to the one in need.

With tongue-in-cheek, Paul used to tell his children: "Eat your vegetables so you can grow up to be big and strong like your mom." The joke was that in comparison with Kitty's short stature, Paul is 6'1" tall. But the truth of that advice is that Kitty always was a strong, energetic person and someone to emulate. Kitty's "big and strong" was her big, loving heart; her strength of character; and her generosity born of a deep love for God and all God's creatures. When Kitty learned that she had Alzheimer's disease, she wanted to tell her children herself. Individually, before a holiday meal, she shared with each child her difficult news. She wanted them to know that despite the upcoming struggles, she understood what was happening to her mind and that she accepted the repercussions. In her strength, she gave her children a model of how to deal with this terrible illness. In the end, Kitty was double-struck with both Alzheimer's and Parkinson's disease. Together, these illnesses ravaged her nervous system and required outside care in a nursing home. Paul visited her daily and the children came whenever possible. Finally, after a last visit from Bill, who lived the furthest away, she let go and moved into God's loving arms.

If we measure Kitty's life by how she lived her life's guiding principles of love for God, family, and community, then it certainly can be said that she was a successful woman. More important, however, Kitty's life was memorable. Each of us in this family has a piece of her in our hearts to prove the depths of her love. May she rest always in God's loving peace.

IV. Eulogy for Ruth B.
(Written For a Post-Funeral Memorial Ceremony)

October 9, 1930 – January 19, 1990

Today we gather to celebrate the life of Ruth Eleanor, who died at sixty years old of a cancer that ravaged her body but not her heart and soul. Ruth's Christian faith was the center of her life. She believed that Christians are reborn daily through their renewed devotion to God, and so she strived to renew her faith each day. Her Bible called her name and Ruth answered especially to "Proverbs," which was for her truly the "Book of Wisdom." So it is appropriate here to see how this book of wisdom guided her life.

Let another praise you—not your own mouth; someone else—not your own lips. (27:2)

Ruth was the third of eight children born to Madeline and John. As the second daughter, her siblings believe she was her daddy's favorite. As the third child, however, she learned early on to care for her brothers and sisters, and she lived that spirit of caring all her life. Ruth was one of those rare people who grew up in a family of eight with all of her siblings remembering her fondly and with love. She was kind to her sisters Sherrill and Daryl and was best friends with her older sister Violet, who purposely failed first grade so they could go through school together. As a teen, she was friendly, fun to be around, and popular in high school. She was a majorette with the high school band and a good dancer. Many boys wanted to be her friend, but for a long time, her special guy was a young man named Homer. Her class voted her the cutest girl.

A lamp from the Lord is the breath of man; it searches through all his inmost being. (20:27)

Ruth's lamp from the Lord was the gift of education—rare in a large working-class family coming out of the Great Depression. She graduated from the Chester Hospital School of Nursing in 1951 and from the Lancaster School of the Bible as a missionary. She chose not to be ordained because doing so would have placed her in a position superior to her husband Millard, who had less education than she. After they both graduated from

170

Lancaster, they began their lives as missionaries. They lived in such remote places as Greeley and Yellow Jacket, Colorado, where she contracted and beat tuberculosis, and Blanchard, Idaho, where she raised her own family.

> When one finds a worthy wife, her value is far beyond pearls. Her husband, entrusting his heart to her, has an unfailing prize.
>
> She brings him good, and not evil, all the days of her life. (31:10-12)

Ruth supported her husband's ministry by walking beside him and caring for the people of his congregations as if they were her own family. At a call from a needing family, she would grab her nursing bag and dash to their home. She nursed children with whooping cough and the measles. She set broken bones for people who couldn't afford a doctor. She even stitched up her neighbors' injured farm animals—keeping hurt pigs and cows from contracting infections that would kill them before they could be used for the family's needs. Ruth gave whatever she had to the people whose souls were entrusted to the pastor and his wife.

> She obtains wool and flax and makes cloth with skillful hands. Like merchant ships, she secures her provisions from afar.
>
> She rises while it is still night, and distributes food to her household. (31:13-15)

A Baptist minister often relies on his congregation's gifts for food and clothing. And, as happens occasionally, the people thought first about having Millard to dinner and providing him with the material goods he needed to be their pastor. Ruth took up the slack and provided for her family—especially during a period of more than a year when Millard had no work. She worked at a doctor's office, as a county nurse traveling from house to house, and at the Newport Nursing Home. In December 1989, one month before her death, Ruth received the Nurse of the Year Award for her efforts.

But Ruth was especially thrifty in caring for her husband and three children—Colleen, Danny, and Kevin. She was an excellent seamstress, making many of her own and her children's clothes. She could knit in the dark, using the many needles necessary to knit the argyle socks that loved ones craved from her. In the summer, her house was a canning factory of various vegetables and fruit. She dried and preserved the meat that her family hunted and the salmon that they fished. She determined

171

that her family would not go hungry despite their own tenuous finances. Her children remember how she would come home from working on Saturday night and then would labor past midnight to prepare the yeast-risen cinnamon buns for Sunday breakfast and homemade rolls for the family dinner. In the morning, she would put the meat in the oven to slow cook while the family was at church; they returned home to the aroma of a hearty Sunday dinner and the anticipation of a weekly family gathering.

Ruth's care for her children was well repaid. Her daughter Colleen followed Ruth's footsteps and became a practical nurse; she had a son who grew up knowing Ruth's kindness. Danny has made a living as a talented carpenter; he has two daughters and a son fortunate enough to have known their grandmother. And Kevin has made a living as a respected iron-worker in bridge construction; the youngest child, Kevin had his own special place in Ruth's heart.

> She reaches out her hands to the poor, and extends her arms to the needy. She fears not the snow for her household; all her charges are doubly clothed. (31:20-21)

Ruth was clever in the ways she handled the near poverty that a pastor's family can experience. She made a sport of Saturday morning yard sales. She prepared for the sales the night before by writing down all the addresses she wanted to visit—some much more than an hour away from their rural, mountain home. She left at 6:00 AM with her friends as companions. Once they were at the yard sale, though, it was every woman for herself! She who found it, got it and neither friendship nor rank of any kind had any privileges. Ruth collected aluminum cans for the deposit money offered for them to add to meager funds at home. Only her sister Violet knew that Ruth hid some of this extra money between the pages of the many books that she loved to read.

Ruth didn't live a fairy-tale life by any means. She experienced sadness and a tragedy that might have destroyed a person of weaker faith. One day, her car broke down and neither Millard nor the children were home to help her out. She called a friend's home and the husband came to help her. As he approached her car, he told her they should move further to the side, out of the path of an oncoming vehicle. The next thing Ruth knew, she was on the ground with a face full of glass. Her neighbor was dead, decapitated by the carelessness of a drunken driver. Ruth recovered, but had physical scars that marred her attractive face. Despite her sadness, her true beauty shined through as she made sure that her friend's family never wanted for food or clothes or the true kindness of a loving friend. Truly, "all her charges" were "doubly clothed."

> She is clothed with strength and dignity, and she laughs at the days to come.

> She opens her mouth in wisdom, and on her tongue is kindly counsel. (31:25-26)

Ruth fought a battle with cancer that began many years earlier. Cancer of the uterus required a hysterectomy; she mourned the loss of the larger family that she wanted, but accepted the loss as a trade-off for being healthy enough to raise her precious children. Years later, breast cancer was caught early, seemingly cured, but then returned as the liver cancer that would take her life. Ruth remained peaceful. She didn't want her family to see her suffer, but her brother Fred and sister Violet visited her anyway because they wanted to be with her a last time. She suffered great pain, but bore it without complaint. When Ruth was able to sleep, she slept in a reclining chair. Otherwise, she spoke quietly with her family, telling them again all the loving things she wanted them to keep in their hearts. And she joked and laughed and was the same Ruth that her high school friends had so much enjoyed. Solid in her faith of a future life with the Lord, Ruth peacefully died on a Thursday in January.

> Her children rise up and praise her; her husband, too, extols her;

> Many are the women of proven worth, but you have excelled them all.

> Charm is deceptive and beauty fleeting; the woman who fears the Lord is to be praised.

> Give her a reward of her labors, and let her works praise her at the city gates. (31:28-31)

A beloved, loving woman who lived a life for others—that's how we remember Ruth these many years later. She found true joy in service to God. Ruth's ashes were placed near her house beside a favorite rock on which she used to sit. Her ashes remained in the yard until her children placed them in a cemetery. Millard died a mere five years later, and, although he had remarried, his ashes were buried with Ruth's. These days, when her children and four grandchildren visit Ruth, they follow an old family tradition and place a stone on the site to signify that they had come to pay their respects. And today this is what we are gathered to do—to pay our respects to an unusually gifted and wise daughter of God.

V. Eulogy for Shelly S.

February 11, 1953 – June 17, 2007

Loving Shelly was easy. Missing Shelly is even easier. But learning to live without Shelly will be the work of a lifetime.

Pretty, petite, and full of life, our Shelly died from cancer after a fiercely fought battle. Her husband Mark and three grown children—Joe, Brian, and Tracey—are realizing that they have to learn to live without the person who has been the bedrock of their lives.

They have to learn to be a family in the vacuum of her absence. If you knew her as they did and as her remaining siblings Stevie, Tim, and Lynn did, then you know that Shelly was practical, considerate, and intensely fair. These traits defined her and profoundly influenced her interactions with the world.

Shelly's practical side has always been apparent. She was self-reliant and hard-working in school. From being a dedicated student at both Immaculate Conception and Towson Catholic High School, she attended the Union Memorial School of Nursing. She "popsicled" with the Good Humor truck in the summer and used the money for her school books and incidentals.

Shelly gravitated toward emergency nursing because it challenged her skills and sustained her practical nature. She liked the pace, the doctors, and the opportunity to use her hard-earned diagnostic skills. Emergency nursing appealed to Shelly's preferences for a clean, uncluttered life. At home, she liked to finish up the business of the day so that the next day would be a truly fresh start; at work, she loved that an ER shift usually presented a clean slate and new patients whose needs would be addressed before the next shift came on. She liked to end her own shift by moving as many patients as possible out of the ER so that her colleagues also would find a clean slate.

Anyone who knew Shelly knew that she was a considerate person. She would check on her favorite ER patients in their hospital rooms to make sure that they were doing okay. Over the years, having spent all her working days at Franklin Square Hospital, Shelly also built relationships with so-called frequent flyers that had chronic health issues like cancer and heart disease. These people loved knowing that Shelly would be there to help them through the ER's sometimes painful routines.

She worked night shift, day shift, 12-hour shifts, holidays, snow days. She missed dinners, parades, and parties, but she never complained. She took care of carnage, crazies, gang members, and politicians. Shelly enjoyed the challenge of cardiac arrests and trauma. She worked long hours, without breaks or meals at times, on her feet and at a run.

Shelly delivered all three children by natural child birth. Mark marvels at her decision and says: "I can understand the idealism of the first, but she knew what was coming with the other two. She did it for their sakes, and to be wholly present when the miracle of their lives entered ours."

At home, Shelly's consideration showed up in small, yet meaningful ways. When her children had a birthday, the first and last piece of cake belonged to the birthday child— no fair cutting away little bits of that last piece for a final nibble either! That last piece of cake was to be as hefty as the first one. At dinner, sometimes she would use the "surprise bowl" for a meal. The lucky person with the decorated bowl got a celebratory kiss and the chance to feel special for a few minutes. Shelly's consideration for others often came at her own expense. She gave more to them and less to herself. She'd buy a shirt for Mark at Sears and shop for a blouse for herself at the consignment shop or Good Will. When handing out chores, she'd choose the worst job for herself, giving her family the ones that they—or she—liked better.

In all ways except for herself, she measured fairly and in equal portions. Mark describes Shelly as having a laser level for an eye and a scale for hands. Both Joe and Brian received the name "Mark" for a middle name because she didn't want to show any possible favoritism in naming the boys. Tracey similarly received Shelly's second name "Ann" for her own middle name.

A promise to Shelly was stronger than a business contract. And even an implied promise like a breezily answered question could become a burden. If Mark or the kids said, "yea, sure" to a request to clean the basement or take out the garbage, Shelly expected that job to be done right away. Even if the job holder actually had answered the request with partial attention or with future intentions of a week, month, or longer, Shelly would become disappointed in what she perceived as a broken promise. In self-protection, her family learned to couch their agreements politically and in conditional language. She could be both steadfastly dedicated and stubbornly resistant.

Shelly loved to dance. She wanted to be good at it but was happy to just get out there. She liked Benny Goodman, the B-52s, and the Violent Femme's "Blister in the Sun"—if it had a beat and made you want to dance, she liked it. She and Mark were taking ballroom dancing classes when she received her initial diagnosis. They wanted to dance together at weddings. Shelly wanted to look like they knew what they were doing, a romantic pair.

She liked to do a "gotcha" where she would play against her own practical and honest reputation by telling some concocted, way-out story and getting someone to believe it for a few minutes. She enjoyed seeing how gullible we could be before she burst out laughing.

The Shelly that we knew brought the entire force of her nature and personality into her fight with cancer. Shortly after having her gallbladder and part of her liver removed at Johns Hopkins, she and Mark walked together daily from the shortest of distances to much longer ones. Despite her physical pain, Shelly was determined to get better. When her rare form of liver cancer proved resistant to therapeutic measures, she had doctors in Baltimore, Georgetown, and San Francisco all working to give her the best palliative care available.

Yes, learning to live without Shelly will be the work of a lifetime—especially for Mark, who sees her as the yin to his yang. He pursued her in high school, pretending to have made a mistake when he drove further than his home the day that she was in his driver's ed car and going to CYO dances that he thought she might attend. In college, while Shelly carefully studied her lessons, he thoughtfully studied her. Together they grew three wonderful children and gardens full of purple cone flowers and butterflies. Although she is gone from Mark's and our physical presence, we can imagine that Shelly is here whenever we hear the soft tunes of wind chimes swaying in the breeze and whenever we look with wonder at the love she has nurtured in our lives. We've told her that we love her, and now the only thing left is to say goodbye.

VI. Memorial Eulogy for Andrew L., age 6 (Written For a Post-Funeral Memorial Ceremony)

January 11, 1986 – January 14, 1992

Today we gather to honor the memory of Andrew L., our son, brother, nephew, cousin, and friend. When Andrew died of leukemia in January 1992—just days past his sixth birthday—we couldn't have imagined that seventeen years would go by so quickly. But quickly doesn't mean thoughtlessly. Like his parents Bill and Anne, we remember Andrew as a loving and loveable little boy.

As a baby, Andrew was an easy child. Anne was blessed with an easy labor and delivery, which is a pleasant surprise to any first-time mother. Together, Anne and Bill enjoyed their baby's milestones: finding his thumb, playing with his toes, rolling over, smiling, laughing, and eventually walking, running, and talking. He was a happy child who also was content simply being quiet and contemplative.

Although he wasn't particularly silly, Andrew liked to giggle and roll around with his parents. He had a sense of humor. When he was just a toddler with his family at the beach, he loved to splash, play, and swim with his daddy. Like most small children, Andrew was drawn to the warmth of the little pools that formed when the ocean tide was going out—he would play in the tidal pools, inviting his family to play with him.

Andrew was a typical five year old when he became sick. He was in pre-school, liked his teacher, and had made some friends. He had a blankie for comfort, built model cars with his daddy, enjoyed watching the *Jungle Story* on video, and had a favorite Mickey Mouse hat. He wore that hat backwards, sideways, frontwards—and he wore it everywhere. Going to the store? He wore that hat. Out for a walk? He wore that hat.

Andrew also enjoyed playing with little toys like model houses, trains, and people. He especially liked playing with Teenage Mutant Ninja Turtle figures. The ninja turtles have been many children's heroes. Like other children between ages four and six, Andrew gravitated towards super heroes who have the magical powers to swoop in to save people from harm. The world is so much bigger than small children and they know they need a protector. But children not only need heroes themselves—they also want to be heroes. And Andrew was no exception. With the wisdom of a child, Andrew's favorite of the Ninja Turtles was Michelangelo. Also called Mikey or Mike, this turtle fit Andrew's developing personality perfectly.

Mike the ninja turtle is a friendly heroic character who is a natural athlete, fast, energetic, and free spirited. Like Mike, before he became sick, Andrew also had a lot of energy and a free-spirited nature. Mike hates confrontation, so he laughs off insults and makes jokes rather than fight with others. Like Mike, Andrew much preferred to play with friends rather than fight or argue. Most importantly, Mike the ninja turtle is highly perceptive regarding the feelings of others and has a strong need to help those who are weaker than himself.

Perhaps in this trait Andrew was most like his favorite turtle hero. For when Andrew was sick, he was especially sweet natured and brave. He never complained and rarely cried. One time, he burst into tears when he learned he had to go to the hospital, but he controlled himself and pulled his tears back before a minute had passed. No one had asked that of him—in fact, Anne and Bill gladly cuddled him through any distress and willingly soothed any tears—but Andrew's sensitivity was for his parents' pain. Instinctively, he knew that taking him to the hospital, especially for painful treatments and bone marrow aspirations, hurt them, too. He acted like a little hero by trying not to cause them more sadness.

Anne and Bill were always there for Andrew, which allowed him to be who he was. They explained to him what leukemia is and how the disease can make people sick, but they also protected him from feeling hopeless by talking about the good things the future would bring when he was healthier. So, like most children, Andrew was able to look forward to going to Disney World, fishing in the springtime, or visiting with his Grandma and Grandpa.

Andrew seemed determined to do the best he could—day in and day out. His days in the hospital could be very lonely, especially in the oncology unit where sometimes he was in isolation because of preparations for bone marrow transplants. So he looked forward to his parents' daily visits, as well as visits from other family members. He would often ask for a gift, but when he received it, the gift hardly held his attention. It was his family that he truly wanted. What hero really wants more than that?

Andrew grew to be sensitive, thoughtful, and deliberate. On the Memorial Day weekend of his fifth year, the family had a gathering. It was a nice day and a warm May afternoon with a buffet lunch on the patio. Everyone was talking, laughing, eating, and drinking happily. Bill recalls that he had a nagging pain of knowing that his beloved son was sick. Then, he looked at Andrew who, in turn, was gazing quietly on each person—smiling from person to person—as if to impart a blessing on them.

When Andrew died, we gathered at the house and at St. Thomas Church, weeping and offering Anne and Bill our support as best we could. They were shattered at the loss of their precious son. Their hopes for his future, like him being next male to inherit the family's antebellum manor, were dashed. They had stepped through the looking glass when he died and since then have seen the world a little differently without Andrew in it.

But as we remember Andrew, let's also recall that Anne and Bill had been so delighted to be his parents that they decided to adopt and raise their beloved daughter Anastasia. The family is changed and has a different shape now, but it still is a family because love of Andrew compelled them to realize they also wanted Anastasia to love. When love is the measure of a family, we know that the family is a success. And so it is with love that we fondly remember Andrew and we continue to offer our support to Anne, Bill, and their dear Anastasia.

VII. Spiritually Focused Eulogy for Paul H.

February 3, 1923 – February 26, 2011

We know that life is a journey. Life as a Christian is a special sort of journey. Jesus asked his disciples to spread His word and to walk the world—taking with them no extra possessions. He told them not to care about how they would eat or where they would sleep because all would be provided to those in His service. He would be our guide and the sole supplier of our needs. In short, Jesus asked for trust in God's benevolence. He asked for active service and not lip service from each of His disciples— indeed, from us. He asked us to be, in essence, love with feet.

Paul walked the world with such love. He spent many years of service with the U.S. Army, traveling the world both alone and with his family. At any point, whether traveling or at home, he was focused on making sure that those who depended on him—family and fellow soldiers—were cared for appropriately. Such journeying always involved service, attention to details, and love. He didn't worry about his own needs because he knew he was safe in God's hands.

Paul worked difficult assignments, some of which he had sworn not to reveal and others that he seemed incapable of finding words to share. He returned to his family with the difficult temperament and occasional rigidity that afflicts many soldiers who have served under the stress of war. And he worked through those difficulties for many years until he came to some kind of peace around them, learning to smile and laugh again, being gentle and silly with grandchildren, and finding joy in the world.

But Paul did not end his life of service with the military. He not only worked in the banking world until retirement, but he took on many, many volunteer positions with local, state, and national committees. He steered committees, helped develop policies, and took responsibility for his place in the world. He did these things not for the many awards that he won but because he cared about the quality of life of others. His love had feet.

Paul was a major force in local community development both in Maryland and here in Delaware. Wherever Paul lived became his home and his neighbors became his family. For example, he served with the Knights of Columbus, and he took on whatever jobs his church required, such as Parish Council work and lectoring. Most intimately, Paul served by bringing the Eucharist to homebound community members before he himself became homebound and needed the grace of others' loving feet.

As we mourn Paul today and for many days to come, please reflect on the many ways that he exemplified Christ's command that we enact love with our feet. What Paul gave to his community, he also gave to his family: a home, financial support, the strength of independence, an understanding of privacy and personal boundaries, the need to volunteer in the service of others, and the intensity of life that comes with loving God and putting faith first. With faith first, none of us needs more than one pair of sandals because God cares for us all in the same ways that He cared for Paul's needs.

Last week, Paul died quietly in bed, and he has joined his beloved Kitty in the joy of God's goodness. I believe he sees us here, recognizes our grief, and smiles knowing that he has already helped to show us the way in our own life's journeys. Personally, I thank God for my Poppa Paul, my father-in-law who taught me much about acceptance, forgiveness, and the power of a smile and a kind, loving touch. Rest in peace, dear Paul, and we shall see you again. You are really and truly done roaming.

VIII. Words of Remembrance for Charles D., Sr. (Written by Son Chuck, 3- Minute Statement, Catholic Mass)

April 3, 1938 - August 30, 2009

For my father and his Father in heaven:

I want to thank my mom for asking me to say a few words about my father. I have practiced this statement a few times, so I can hopefully do it without crying. I want to tell you about my fathers' life and I want to tell you about the last thing I learned in his presence.

My father was clearly a great man. I can't really get too specific here, but it is enough to say that he did more things right than wrong and he made very few crucial mistakes. Life has many, many pitfalls. Some people find every single one of them and others miss them all. It amazes me to say that my dad missed them all. He did the right things at the right time and had the right plan. My father led by example. He did not preach or judge people for doing the wrong thing. He just tried to get them to watch him do it right.

There is a famous piece of scripture that defines the fruit of a spirit-filled life in the book of Galatians, Chapter 5. I will just paraphrase here. You will know someone lives in the spirit when they have love, joy, peace, patience, kindness, goodness, faithfulness, gentleness, and self-control. This is love that surpasses all understanding, an endless love that comes from God and joy and peace that surpass all understanding, even in the face of enormous conflicts and storms. When you look at my father's life (especially the last 10 years of his life), you have to admit, these were plentiful. Peace in times of turmoil. Kindness, goodness, and self-control in times of strife. Patience when you were off the path. And always a faithful love that never fails.

These fruits are evidence of a life well lived and have surrounded my mother and my father for many years, and you don't have to look hard to find them.

So how did they do it? If I had one question to ask of my father, it would be how did you do that all of these years? How did you always make the right decision?

I did not know this answer until the last day of my dad's life. On Sunday, there was a Mass at my parents' house in Forest Hill. This has been a somewhat regular occurrence over the last few months. Father Victor was the celebrant. Some of you were there for that Mass. My father was there until the end of that Mass. The readings were the appropriate readings from the 22nd Sunday in ordinary time. The Old Testament reading was from Deuteronomy and it spelled out the laws. Debbie read it. The psalm read by

> Robbie was more about the law and the right decisions. I stumbled through the New Testament reading from James regarding hearing the Word and doing the Word and the Gospel was from Mark on the

spirit of the Word and law. Fr Victor interpreted it all in a beautiful but brief homily.

I have been to so many Masses with my dad over a lifetime, and I wish I would have caught this message before. But I don't think it would have had the same significance for me at any other time. I hope I am not taking anything away from Fr. Victor when I say that I feel that his message and the message of the church that day came to me from my dad. My dad, who could not speak and could barely breathe, answered my last question with the help of God and many angels. I heard him say, "It's all about faith."

You can't do the right thing and hope faith develops. You need faith to do the right thing. Put another way, only in the context of faith can you truly hear the Word and understand the law enough to make the right decisions. So the last message I heard in the presence of my father was: "You have to have faith first before you make decisions otherwise you're just shooting in the dark." Like all truths, it seems so simple. I should have been able to guess it before. Faith is not an end; it is not a fruit of the spirit. It is the means to the end and the source of the fruit.

My father was a great man, led by great faith to a love that never fails. If we all believe as my father did, we all will be seeing him again. So I am sure he would ask that you let your tears be tears of joy for him and for the love of God whom he faithfully served his entire life.

Thank you.

IX. In Memoriam of Alan H. Avram ben Mordecai (Jewish Hesped)

We are here to say our final farewell to Alan H., finally taken from the loving arms of his family at the age of almost 80 years. Those who are here feel a keen sense of loss. One who is deeply loved is to be sorely missed; that is the way of the world. We have lost a husband, a brother, a father, a grandfather, a good friend and a valiant citizen.

And it is fitting that we are in this room for this moment of remembrance and salute. Woodlands is the congregation that Alan helped build. Except for his vision and his efforts, this place would simply not exist. He is forever a part of this community, and his personality is reflected in the fabric of who and what we are.

Let me begin by telling you a story. It was the 1960's, a time of social restlessness and change. Alan H. had an idea. He wanted to create a new synagogue, a dynamic and democratic Jewish institution that would reflect the idealism that was in the air. I have heard that he carried the briefcase with the paperwork for this enterprise with him on the train, and every day he would be seen going over it, during the ride into and out of Manhattan.

Alan had imagination; he had fire, and worked hard to see that his visions would come into being. He was one of that generation of tough New York kids, a Bronx High School of Science and NYU graduate, one of many dynamic men and women who combined the energy and drive of youth with the wise and humane world view of a social reformer. He was a man ideally suited to build and create. Alan was brilliant, focused and extremely hard working. First he ran an extremely successful insurance business, and in the meantime, turned to creating a synagogue.

Alan gathered some other enthusiasts and called a meeting. He put out a flyer across the area which asked, "Are you tired of going to your parent's synagogue for the Holidays?" Come and build a new synagogue, it beckoned. Eighty people came to that first meeting, people from four different school districts, from five or more different municipalities. It was clear that this was to be a community synagogue, and it would take a person with big ideas and great ability to bring it into being. Alan was such a man.

Alan showed traits in his role as president that could be seen in all the aspects of his life. He was enthusiastic and hard driving when working on a project. He showed a sense of humor and the ability to get others to follow his lead. He could think fast, and make decisions in the spur of the moment. When others were indecisive, he was definite, and would push through and lead on to action. He was the right man for the moment, and we can thank Alan that Woodlands is here today.

Today, Woodlands is a place that has a national, even an international reputation. We are known for our broad tent of inclusion, our sympathy for the individual and for a commitment to social action. We are free thinking and liberal with an appreciation for tradition. We are wont to say that community is our middle name; we are without cliques and exclusive clubs. We are tolerant of individual opinions and are fussy about details. We are energetic and creative, and bold to try new initiatives. I suggest that all these things are traits that Alan had, and it is no surprise that people who believe in those things have found a home in this community.

Our Rabbis say that a man has many names, for he has many facets. There is the name you are given. There is the name that you make for yourself. There is the name that your friends call you, and the name your foes use, as well. There is also the name the angels call, and the name God remembers.

In all these names, Alan's identity is to be written in large letters. He contributed to the world around him with fierce vitality and spirited achievement. He was also gentle and vulnerable. I will always remember his soft smile of pride when he stood here at Woodlands and held our Torah scroll with other presidents on Kol Nidrei evening. He was part of a line, and he had started it all.

His legacy will stand the long passage of time. Our respect for Alan, and our love for him, will never fade, and his name will be an eternal blessing.

T'hei nishmato ts'rorah bitsror hachayim.

So may it be.

Appendix B

Example Words and Poetry for Blessing and Honoring

Words of Blessing

"In Memory of My Sister" (Beth Hewett)

When we are faced with death, we tend to review our lives in connection with the one we loved. This is a good thing to do so that we can grieve and mourn well.

When our loved one has died an uncomplicated death where the illness or the body's wounds are sudden or unconnected to their actions, it may be easier to open our torn hearts to our emotions. But when the death is in any way complicated by one's life, it is harder to disconnect the loss of our loved one with his or her own actions.

Kathy carried in her heart a deep sadness and we can only guess at its source, but we cannot deny that she tried hard to fight it. However, over the years, her battles with alcohol and depression led her to alienate many of us. And, so, tonight we may wonder who it is that we are mourning.

To be clear, we are mourning Murphy's wife; Zeke and Rachael's mother; Daryl's daughter; Beth, Michael, and Mary Ann's sister; our aunt, cousin, friend, and co-worker. Kathy touched everyone's life here, so she is deeply on our minds and hearts tonight.

It might be hard to separate this Kathy of our lives with the woman who drowned in a painful addiction. But alcohol and emotional illness are not the essence of Kathy, merely her sad companions through her last years. Although she may not have been able to access these feelings easily during those years, she deeply loved her husband, son, daughter, and mother.

Let us join in a blessing of Kathy that will enable us to begin our mourning and healing by recalling the essence of Kathy:

Please close your eyes and imagine her at her loveliest and most open. See her smile and watch her blush as she found someone's attention unexpectedly on her. Share in her joy at her wedding and the birth of her two beloved children. Watch her dance with wild abandon at a rock concert or deftly pick a crab while telling a funny story. Listen to her sexy, throaty laugh as she joked about someone saying "fort routey" rather than "route forty" or as she watched her children play in the pool with their cousins. Taste the delicious and nourishing food she enjoyed making for others.

This is the Kathy we want to remember. Now, with this beloved Kathy firmly fixed in your minds, please bless her and her life by repeating these words after me. In doing so, you will lock her true essence into your hearts.

Kathy, you are incredibly loveable.

Kathy, you always have been incredibly loveable.

Kathy, you always will be incredibly loveable.

Kathy, your true nature is love.

Thank you.

Finally, I'd like to close with this song chosen especially to speak to Kathy's spirit. Kathy sang "Muskrat Love" for me at my wedding, but I am too broken hearted to try to sing to her tonight. In keeping with our theme of "going home," John Denver will end our service with "The Wings to Fly Us Home."

Poetry of Blessing

I. "On Pain" (Kahlil Gibran)

Your pain is the breaking of the shell that encloses your understanding.

Even as the stone of the fruit must break, that its heart may stand in the sun, so must you know pain.

And could you keep your heart in wonder at the daily miracles of your life, your pain would not seem less wondrous than your joy;

And you would accept the seasons of your heart, even as you have always accepted the seasons that pass over your fields.

And you would watch with serenity through the winters of your grief. Much of your pain is self-chosen.

It is the bitter potion by which the physician within you heals your sick self.

Therefore trust the physician, and drink his remedy in silence and tranquility:

For his hand, though heavy and hard, is guided by the tender hand of the Unseen,

And the cup he brings, though it burn your lips, has been fashioned of the clay which the Potter has moistened with His own sacred tears.

II. "On Death" (Kahlil Gibran)

Then Almitra spoke, saying, "We would ask now of Death." And he said:

"You would know the secret of death. But how shall you find it unless you seek it in the heart of life? The owl whose night-bound eyes are blind unto the day cannot unveil the mystery of light. If you would indeed behold the spirit of death, open your heart wide unto the body of life. For life and death are one, even as the river and the sea are one. In the depth of your hopes and desires lies your silent knowledge of the beyond; And like seeds dreaming beneath the snow your heart dreams of spring. Trust the dreams, for in them is hidden the gate to eternity. Your fear of death is but the trembling of the shepherd when he stands before the king whose hand is to be laid upon him in honour. Is the shepherd not joyful beneath his trembling, that he shall wear the mark of the king? Yet is he not more mindful of his trembling? For what is it to die but to stand naked in the wind and to melt into the sun? And what is to cease breathing, but to free the breath from its restless tides, that it may rise and expand and seek God unencumbered? Only when you drink from the river of silence shall you indeed sing. And when you have reached the mountain top, then you shall begin to climb. And when the earth shall claim your limbs, then shall you truly dance.

III. "Prayer of St. Francis of Assisi"

Lord, make me an instrument of your peace.
Where this is hatred, let me sow love;
Where there is injury, pardon;
Where there is doubt, faith; Where
there is despair, hope; Where there
is darkness, light And where there
is sadness, joy. O Divine Master,
grant that I may not so much seek to be consoled as to console;
to be understood as to understand;
to be loved as to love.
For it is in giving that we receive;
It is in pardoning that we are pardoned,
And it is in dying that we are born to eternal life.

IV. "Death Is Nothing at All" (Canon Henry Scott Holland)

Death is nothing at all.
I have only slipped away to the next room.
I am I and you are you.
Whatever we were to each other,
That, we still are.

Call me by my old familiar name.
Speak to me in the easy way
which you always used.
Put no difference into your tone.
Wear no forced air of solemnity or sorrow.

Laugh as we always laughed
at the little jokes we enjoyed together.
Play, smile, think of me. Pray for me.
Let my name be ever the household word
that it always was.
Let it be spoken without effect.
Without the trace of a shadow on it.

Life means all that it ever meant.
It is the same that it ever was.
There is absolute unbroken continuity.

Why should I be out of mind
because I am out of sight?

I am but waiting for you.
For an interval.
Somewhere. Very near.
Just around the corner.

All is well.

Nothing is past; nothing is lost.
One brief moment and all will be as it was before only better,
infinitely happier and forever we will all be one together with Christ.

[Alternate ending:]
Nothing is past; nothing is lost.
One brief moment and all will be as it was before.
How we shall laugh at the trouble of parting when we meet again!

V. "Crossing the Bar" (Alfred, Lord Tennyson)

Sunset and evening star,
And one clear call for me!
And may there be no moaning of the bar,
When I put out to sea,

But such a tide as moving seems asleep,
Too full for sound and foam,
When that which drew from out the boundless deep
Turns again home.
Twilight and evening bell,
And after that the dark!
And may there be no sadness of farewell,
When I embark;

For though from out our bourne of Time and Place
The flood may bear me far,
I hope to see my Pilot face to face
When I have crossed the bar.

VI. "I Thank Thee God, That I Have Lived" (Elizabeth Craven)

I thank thee God, that I have lived
In this great world and known its many joys:
The songs of birds, the strongest sweet scent of hay,
And cooling breezes in the secret dusk;
The flaming sunsets at the close of day,
Hills and the lovely, heather-covered moors;
Music at night, and the moonlight on the sea,
The beat of waves upon the rocky shore
And wild white spray, flung high in ecstasy;
The faithful eyes of dogs, and treasured books,
The love of Kin and fellowship of friends
And all that makes life dear and beautiful.

I thank Thee too, that there has come to me
A little sorrow and sometimes defeat,
A little heartache and the loneliness
That comes with parting and the words 'Good-bye';
Dawn breaking after weary hours of pain,
When I discovered that night's gloom must yield
And morning light break through to me again.
Because of these and other blessings poured
Unasked upon my wondering head,
Because I know that there is yet to come
An even richer and more glorious life,
And most of all, because Thine only Son
Once sacrificed life's loveliness for me,
I thank Thee, God, that I have lived.

VII. "They That Love Beyond the World" (William Penn)

They that love beyond the world cannot be separated by it,
death cannot kill what never dies.
Nor can spirits ever be divided that love
and live in the same divine principle,
the root and record of their friendship.
If absence be not death, neither is theirs.
Death is but crossing the world, as friends do the seas;
they live in one another still.
For they must needs be present,

that love and live in that which is omnipresent.
In this divine glass, they see face to face;
and their converse is free as well as pure.
This is the comfort of friends,
that though they may be said to die,
yet their friendship and society are,
in the best sense, ever present, because immortal.

VIII. "You Know How Little Time We Have to Stay" (Omar Khayyam)

You know how little time we have to stay,
And once departed, may return no more.
Ah, my Beloved, fill the Cup that clears
Today of past Regrets and future fears.

Ah, make the most of what we yet may spend,
Before we too into the Dust descend;
Dust unto Dust, and under Dust, to lie,
Sans Wine, Sans Song, sans Singer and sans End!

The Moving Finger writes; and having writ,
Moves on: nor all thy Piety nor Wit
Shall lure it back to cancel half a line
Nor all your Tears wash out a Word of it.

IX. You Know How Little Time We Have to Stay (Omar Khayyam)

You know how little time we have to stay,
And once departed, may return no more.
Ah, my Beloved, fill the Cup that clears
Today of past Regrets and future fears.
Ah, make the most of what we yet may spend,
Before we too into the Dust descend;
Dust unto Dust, and under Dust, to lie,
Sans Wine, Sans Song, sans Singer and sans End!
The Moving Finger writes; and having writ,
Moves on: nor all thy Piety nor Wit
Shall lure it back to cancel half a line
Nor all your Tears wash out a Word of it.

Poetry of Honoring

I. "Because I Could Not Stop for Death" (Emily Dickinson)

Because I could not stop for Death
He kindly stopped for me;
The carriage held but just ourselves
And Immortality.

We slowly drove, he knew no haste, And I had put away
My labor, and my leisure too, For his civility.

We passed the school where children played,
Their lessons scarcely done;
We passed the fields of gazing grain,
We passed the setting sun.

We paused before a house that seemed
A swelling of the ground;
The roof was scarcely visible,
The cornice but a mound.

Since then 'tis centuries; but each
Feels shorter than the day
I first surmised the horses' heads
Were toward eternity.

II. "To My Dear and Loving Husband" (Anne Bradstreet)

If ever two were one, then surely we.
If ever man were loved by wife, then thee;
If ever wife was happy in a man,
Compare with me, ye women, if you can.
I prize thy love more than whole mines of gold,
Or all the riches that the East doth hold.
My love is such that rivers cannot quench,
Nor aught by love from thee give recompense.
Thy love is such I can no way reply;
The heavens reward thee manifold, I pray.
Then while we live, in love let's so persevere,
That when we live no more we may live ever.

III. "Remember Me" (author unknown)

To the living, I am gone,
To the sorrowful, I will never return,
To the angry, I was cheated,
But to the happy, I am at peace,
And to the faithful, I have never left.

I cannot speak, but I can listen.
I cannot be seen, but I can be heard.
So as you stand upon a shore gazing at a beautiful sea–
As you look upon a flower and admire its simplicity–
Remember me.

Remember me in your heart:
Your thoughts, and your memories,
Of the times we loved,
The times we cried,
The times we fought,
The times we laughed.

For if you always think of me, I will never have gone.

IV. "Sonnet X" (John Donne)

Death be not proud, though some have called thee
Mighty and dreadful, for, thou art not so,
For, those, whom thou think'st, thou dost overthrow,
Die not, poor death, nor yet canst thou kill me.
From rest and sleep, which but thy pictures bee,
Much pleasure, then from thee, much more must flow,
And soonest our best men with thee doe go,
Rest of their bones, and soul's delivery.
Thou art slave to Fate, Chance, kings, and desperate men,
And dost with poison, war, and sicknesses dwell,
And poppy, or charms can make us sleep as well,
And better than thy stroke; why swell'st thou then?
One short sleep past, we wake eternally,
And death shall be no more; Death, thou shalt die.

V. "I Am Standing Upon the Seashore" (Henry Van Dyke)

I am standing upon the seashore. A ship, at my side,
spreads her white sails to the moving breeze and starts
for the blue ocean. She is an object of beauty and strength.
I stand and watch her until, at length, she hangs like a speck
of white cloud just where the sea and sky come to mingle with each other.

Then, someone at my side says, "There, she is gone"

Gone where?

Gone from my sight. That is all. She is just as large in mast,
hull and spar as she was when she left my side.
And, she is just as able to bear her load of living freight to her destined
port.

Her diminished size is in me -- not in her.
And, just at the moment when someone says, "There, she is gone,"
there are other eyes watching her coming, and other voices
ready to take up the glad shout, "Here she comes!"

And that is dying...

Death comes in its own time, in its own way.
Death is as unique as the individual experiencing it.

VI. "The Road Not Taken" (Robert Frost)

Two roads diverged in a yellow wood,
And sorry I could not travel both
And be one traveler, long I stood
And looked down one as far as I could
To where it bent in the undergrowth;

Then took the other, as just as fair,
And having perhaps the better claim,
Because it was grassy and wanted wear;
Though as for that, the passing there
Had worn them really about the same,

And both that morning equally lay
In leaves no step had trodden black.
Oh, I kept the first for another day!
Yet knowing how way leads on to way,
I doubted if I should ever come back.

I shall be telling this with a sigh
Somewhere ages and ages hence:
Two roads diverged in a wood, and I—
I took the one less traveled by,
And that has made all the difference.

VII. "To an Athlete Dying Young" (A. E. Housman)

The time you won your town the race
We chaired you through the market-place;
Man and boy stood cheering by,
And home we brought you shoulder-high.

Today, the road all runners come,
Shoulder-high we bring you home,
And set you at your threshold down,
Townsman of a stiller town.

Smart lad, to slip betimes away
From fields where glory does not stay,
And early though the laurel grows
It withers quicker than the rose.

Eyes the shady night has shut
Cannot see the record cut,
And silence sounds no worse than cheers
After earth has stopped the ears.

Now you will not swell the rout
Of lads that wore their honours out,
Runners whom renown outran
And the name died before the man.

So set, before its echoes fade,
The fleet foot on the sill of shade,
And hold to the low lintel up
The still-defended challenge-cup.

And round that early-laurelled head
Will flock to gaze the strengthless dead,
And find unwithered on its curls
The garland briefer than a girl's.

VIII. "Requiem" (Robert Louis Stevenson)

Under the wide and starry sky,
Dig the grave and let me lie.
Glad did I live and gladly die,
And I laid me down with a will.

This be the verse you gave for me
Here he lies where he longed to be;
Home is the sailor, home from the sea,
And the hunter home from the hill.

Appendix C

Eulogy Writing Guide

This *Eulogy Writing Guide* can be removed from your book. Use it to:

- Gather information about the deceased
- Make decisions about what details to use in the eulogy
- Decide how you'll organize the eulogy

Refer back to chapters 3, 4, and 7 and appendixes A and B for examples of how to do these writing tasks.

Finding Good Words for the Traditional Eulogy

Step 1: Talk with family members

Family members, as well as close friends, usually have memories of their loved ones that they'd like to share. They also have different insights and perspectives about the deceased. While they might not be the best people to write the eulogy, they are the best people to provide its basic content.

Step 2: Gently elicit information from family members

There are at least three kinds of information that you should try to get:

- Factual details
- Biographical stories
- Character qualities

Factual Details

- The person's full name and whether a middle name or nickname should be used
- Dates of birth and death
- Date/s of marriage/s
- Names and number of children or siblings, if any
- Level of education and the name of the school/s
- Current or past career/s
- Any other details that the family wants to provide.

In the space provided below, record some of the factual details about the deceased that bereaved family and friends might want in the eulogy.

Although some factual details are important to the eulogy, you don't need to include every date or person in the deceased's life. By starting your research with such a list, you'll be able to figure out the critical ones for the eulogy by moving into the second kind of information— biographical stories.

Factual Details

Biographical Stories

Biographical stories include the family and friends' memories and favorite anecdotes about the deceased. Here, you might ask each person for a story about the loved one:

- What is your favorite memory of your daddy?
- When you saw your mom or talked to her on the phone, was there something you could always count on her to say or do?
- What did you love best about your little brother?
- Your sister had six children and they all seemed so happy with her. Did she ever tell you how she managed to raise them so well?
- I know you only got to see your cousin in the summertime at the farm. What did you like best about seeing her for the first time each year?
- What would Sam's college friends say about him as a fraternity brother?

Just like the factual details, not every biographical memory needs to go into a eulogy. But it's helpful to have something representative to tell in relation to key family members, friends, and co-workers who will be at the services.

Use the space provided below to record some of the biographical stories that you learn from the family and friends of the deceased. Although you don't need to make any decisions yet about which ones to include in the eulogy, you might place a check by those anecdotes that best illustrate the deceased. The third kind of information, character qualities, will help you to make your decisions.

Biographical Stories

Character Qualities

Now that you have some factual and biographical details about the deceased, consider what qualities or characteristics people most admire about him or her. This information will help you to choose which facts or biographical details to include in the eulogy. It also will help you to develop a primary theme.

The virtues and noble activities that have guided this person's life also will guide and shape the eulogy. These qualities are essential to understanding the most endearing characteristics of people. And, these qualities are the most enduring ones that people will remember years from now about your loved one.

Virtues are character qualities that demonstrate moral goodness or righteousness. Although none of us has lived a perfect life, most of us have acquired one or more:

- Justice
- Courage
- Self-control
- Generosity
- Fairness
- Gentleness
- Integrity
- Patience
- Passion
- Respect
- Commitment
- Dependability
- Selflessness
- Thoughtfulness
- Life-based wisdom
- Knowledge-based wisdom

Noble activities are actions that we recognize as "good" for family, friends, local community, or greater society. These noble actions matter beyond the individual:

- Actions that are most useful to others
- Honorable deeds
- Unselfish behavior
- Acts of self-sacrifice, justice, and kindness
- Acts that bring credit to oneself or one's family in the eyes of the community and greater society

When used to "discover" what to say about the deceased, these virtues and noble activities help to explore the person's life.

Using the space provided below for notes, write some of the virtues that you think most exemplify this person. Why or how did you see these qualities? Write out some of these ideas. Do the same thing for noble activities. Place checks by the ones that you think are most important to talk about. Try to get family members' input, too.

Character Qualities

Virtues:

Noble activities:

Step 3: Get ready to write the eulogy

In this final step, begin to pull your notes together. Use what you've learned from family members and friends, as well as your own sense of the deceased. In addition, you can refer to example eulogies in appendix A.

Look back to the biographical stories and character qualities lists. First, read the checked notes to see whether you still want to talk about these things. Then, look at the notes without checks to see whether you've missed something important. Connect the personal details, biographical stories, and character qualities that seem to go together. See what themes emerge from your notes.

Using the space provided below, write the connections that you see among the personal details, biographical stories, and character qualities that you want to discuss.

Intersection of Personal Details, Biographical Stories, and Character Qualities (Themes)

Finding Good Words for Blessing and Honoring

Difficult Relationships and Situations

What good words can you say when you're conflicted about the person who has died? How can you say good things about the deceased if you haven't reached peace about whatever caused the problem? How can you write a eulogy about someone you generally didn't admire or like or who didn't seem virtuous and noble?

First, you don't need to be the person to write that eulogy. Get someone else to do it. When you're both grieving the loss and feeling upset with the deceased, it can be especially hard to find, let alone write, the best about that person.

In fact, the traditional eulogy may not be the right venue for honoring the memory of certain individuals. However, even difficult relationships can lend themselves to traditional eulogies. Any time that a virtue exists that can be praised, try to write a traditional eulogy.

Here, the difference between the ideas of praising, blessing, and honoring become important because even when we find it difficult to praise a life, we can bless or honor the deceased with good words and love. In other words, we can dislike what the person has done while still loving the person—or at least acknowledging his or her common human nature in a nonjudgmental way. Praise expressed in a eulogy is about the deceased; blessings and honoring are expressed *for* or *to* the deceased (and the bereaved). As opposed to praising, the act of blessing or honoring is non-judgmental. Everyone can be memorialized because of our shared human nature.

How to Bless and Honor

There are a variety of ways that we can memorialize people who are difficult to praise in a traditional eulogy.

First, make the eulogy short. Using steps 1 and 2 listed above, talk with family members and gently seek information about the deceased. People are likely to recall something good about this person in childhood or adolescence—before life's challenges brought him or her down. If there's a virtue that emerges, use it to develop a more traditional eulogy. If not, try telling a biographical story that shows the innocence or delight of a child. Remember the family needs to hear these good words.

Second, decide whether you'd like to bless or honor this person.

There are many examples of blessings available in books and on the Internet. For example, traditional funeral blessings that lay people often use include participatory readings, psalms, and spiritual poetry. See appendix B for examples.

Other ideas for blessings and honors include:

- Leading an opportunity for everyone to state a good wish for the deceased while lighting a candle or taking/giving a rose or other flower
- Giving the mourners a memento of the deceased like a prayer card, handmade butterfly, or copy of a poem
- Playing a special piece of music and providing the lyrics to the gathered people
- Singing a well-known song together.

Organizing the Eulogy

Like any other speech, the typical eulogy has at least three parts: (1) an introduction that suggests a theme; (2) a body section of a narrative story or stories, illustrative details, and examples; and (3) a conclusion to draw everything together.

Introductions

What does the introduction generally do? It might:

- Give specifics about the deceased like the name, age, and/or marital and parenting status
- Say something about the occasion and purpose for the eulogy
- Highlight the deceased's main virtues

- Indicate how the eulogy is organized
- Address your relationship to the deceased

The Body of the Eulogy

The body of the eulogy is a narration of the deceased's life. It is the most crucial part of the speech. This is where you would use the biographical stories that you gathered earlier. There are various ways to arrange the body of the eulogy. The choice you make depends on the story that you want to tell. See Chapter 4 for examples of each organizational strategy.

Organizational strategies include:

- Chronology, or timeframes within a person's life, that demonstrate how one has grown or developed:
    - Earliest to most recent years
    - Recent to earliest years (reverse chronology)
- Events that the deceased experienced or that he or she caused, as well as the effects of these events:
    - Critical events that shaped the person
    - Deeds that the person performed
- Influence on others, including the world at large:
    - A person's influence on family and friends
    - How people will remember the deceased
- Themes that represent important virtues:
    - How the deceased learned these virtues
    - How the virtues were demonstrated in the deceased's life

Conclusions

A eulogy needs a conclusion that provides a sense of closure and emotional satisfaction about the deceased's life. The eulogy's conclusion symbolizes that a life has ended, just as it signals to the gathered mourners that the next part of the ceremony will begin.

There are patterns for concluding the eulogy, such as:

- Explaining why the mourners should think favorably about the deceased
- Asking questions, making comparisons, or otherwise reminding the mourners of the loved one's chief praise-worthy characteristics
- Encouraging people to emulate these attributes, which is a way of minimizing more negative ones
- Calling on a common conception of God or a Higher Power for consolation and blessing
- Using emotional cues that move the audience to react with sorrow, pity, indignation, and even laughter

Whenever you need to, refer back to chapters 3, 4, 7, and appendixes A and B as you write the eulogy. Then, review chapter 5 for tips about delivering the eulogy.

About the Cover Artist

Moonjoo Lee is a graduate of the Hongik University, a noted art college in Seoul, South Korea. She has won awards and scholarships for her artwork. Moonjoo's art is characterized by a rich integration of subject, color, and texture.

About the Book Cover

The dragonfly begins its life as a nymph water bug. As it matures, it morphs into a beautiful four-winged insect. In this new body, it cannot return to the water to share with other water bugs how it has transformed; the water, like death, acts as a veil to separate one creature from the other. Like the butterfly, the dragonfly symbolizes change of life, new beginnings, and in some traditions, it is believed to be the soul of the deceased flying free in a new life.

The stone wall in this painting is the artist's representation of the *Wailing Wall* in Jerusalem.